AA Explorer
THE WEST COUNTRY

AA Publishing

Text and illustrations taken from the series *Explore Britain's...*, first published by the Automobile Association and the Daily Telegraph in 1993 and 1995:

Explore Britain's Castles by Elizabeth Cruwys and Beau Riffenburg
Explore Britain's Coastline by Richard Cavendish
Explore Britain's Country Gardens by Michael Wright
Explore Britain's Historic Houses by Penny Hicks
Explore Britain's National Parks by Roland Smith
Explore Britain's Steam Railways by Anthony Lambert
Explore Britain's Villages by Susan Gordon

Published by AA Publishing, a trading name of Automobile Association Developments Limited, whose registered office is Norfolk House, Priestley Road, Basingstoke, Hampshire RG24 9NY. Registered Number 1878835.

A catalogue record for this book is available from the British Library.

ISBN 0 7495 1299 7

Colour origination by L. C. Repro & Sons Ltd, Aldermaston, England
Printed and bound in Italy by Tipolitografia G. Canale & C.S.p.A. – Turin

The contents of this book are believed correct at the time of printing. Nevertheless, the Publishers cannot accept responsibility for errors or omissions, or for changes in details given.

Acknowledgements:

AA PHOTO LIBRARY B/Cover: a S. & O. Mathews, b F. Stephenson, c S. L. Day, d H. Williams, e E. Meacher, f K. Paterson; 1 N. Ray; 3 P. Baker; 7 A. Lawson; 8, 9 A. J. Hopkins; 10/11 A. Baker; 12, 13, N. Ray; 14 R. Moss; 15 A. Baker; 16, 17 H. Williams; 22 S. & O. Mathews; 24/5, 25 R. Moss; 26 T. Teegan; 27 S. & O. Mathews; 28 N. Ray; 29 A. Lawson; 30/1, 32, 33 J. Wyand; 34, 35, 36, 37, 38 A. Lawson; 39 J. Wyand; 40, 41 A. Lawson; 42/3 V. Sinhal; 45 A. Lawson; 46 T. Teegan; 47 A. Lawson; 48 R. Hayman; 49 R. Moss; 50 , 51a, 51b N. Ray; 52, 53, R. Moss; 54, 55 A. Lawson; 56, 57 R. Moss; 58/9 T. Teegan; 60 A. Lawson; 61 H. Williams; 63 A. Lawson; 65 S. & O. Mathews; 66 T. Teegan; 67, 68 H. Williams; 69 A. Lawson; 71 S. & O. Mathews; 72, 73, 74, 75 P. Baker; 76/7, 77 S. L. Day; 78, 79a, 79b, 80, 81a, 81b A. Baker; 83 R. Czaja; 84, 85 A. Baker; 86 T. Teegan; 87 P. Baker; 88, 89a, 89b, 90, 91a, 91b A. Baker; 92, 93, 94/5, 95 N. Ray; 96 E. Meacher; 97, 98, 99a, 99b, 100, 101 A. Baker; 102 W. Voysey; 103 R. Newton; 105 N. Ray; 106/7 R. Czaja; 107 E. Meacher; 108, 109 H. Williams; 110, 111 N. Ray; 112/3 M. Birkitt; 113 R. Newton; 114 A. Baker; 115 A. Lawson; 116/7, 117 A. Souter; 118, 119 A. Baker; 120, 121 A. Lawson
THE NATIONAL TRUST 124, 125, 126, 127; STOURTON HOUSE GARDEN 104/5; TREBAH GARDEN TRUST 18, 19; TRESCO ABBEY GARDENS 20, 21a, b; ANDY WILLIAMS PHOTO LIBRARY F/Cover Bedruthen Steps

CONTENTS

THE WEST COUNTRY

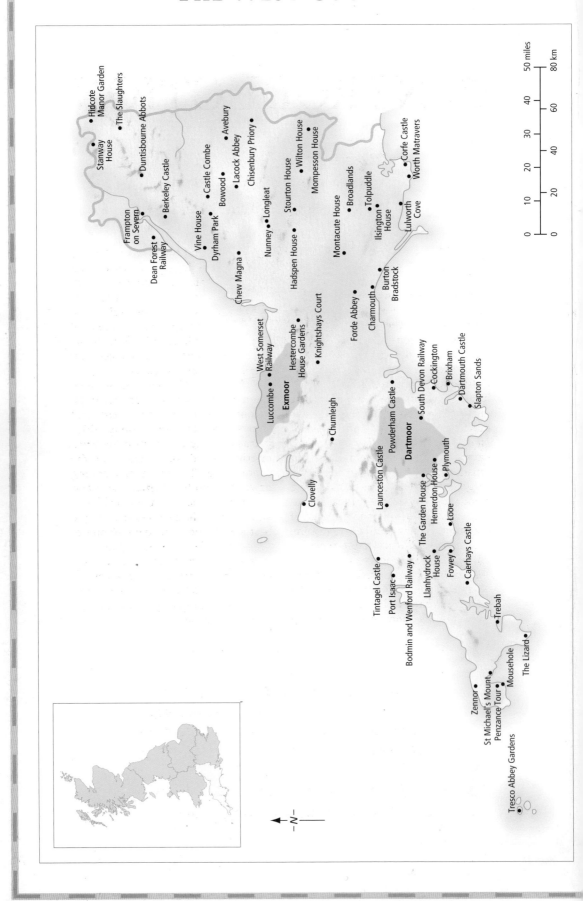

Hidcote Manor Garden
The Slaughters
Stanway House
Duntisbourne Abbots
Berkeley Castle
Castle Combe
Avebury
Lacock Abbey
Chisenbury Priory
Bowood
Wilton House
Mompesson House
Corfe Castle
Worth Matravers
Vine House
Stourton House
Broadlands
Frampton on Severn
Dyrham Park
Nunney
Longleat
Tolpuddle
Dean Forest Railway
Chew Magna
Hadspen House
Ilsington House
Lulworth Cove
Montacute House
Forde Abbey
Burton Bradstock
Charmouth
Knightshays Court
West Somerset Railway
Hestercombe House Gardens
Exmoor
Luccombe
Chumleigh
Dartmouth Castle
Cockington
Brixham
Slapton Sands
South Devon Railway
Powderham Castle
Dartmoor
Launceston Castle
Plymouth
Hemerdon House
The Garden House
Looe
Clovelly
Tintagel Castle
Port Isaac
Bodmin and Wenford Railway
Llanhydrock House
Fowey
Caerhays Castle
Trebah
The Lizard
Zennor
St Michael's Mount
Penzance Tour
Mousehole
Tresco Abbey Gardens

0   10   20   30   40   50 miles
0   20   40   60   80 km

— N —

𝒥NTRODUCTION

✦

I think she was the most beautiful lady
That ever was in the West Country

Walter de la Mare, from 'Epitaph'

'Go west, young man' – sound advice indeed. The West Country of Britain is the stuff of legends and adventure, from the wild coasts of Cornwall to the gentle sophistication of the Cotswolds. Steeped in history, you can take your pick of prehistoric fossil hunting on Dorset's beaches or wandering the region's many stately homes. For centuries a haven of inspiration for writers and artists, whether drawn to the bleak ruggedness of Dartmoor or the rolling moorlands, wooded valleys and beautiful coastline of Exmoor. An area of the country that never fails to inspire, the West is rich in picture-postcard villages, contrasting coastlines with craggy cliffs, bustling fishing communities and sleepy sheltered ports. Its temperate climate has resulted in a splendour of country gardens. Its long

and proud history leaves a legacy of castles and stately homes, both ancient and modern, dramatic and genteel – from the spectacular setting of St Michael's Mount to the sedate aristocracy of Bowood House .

No less than nine colourful and scenic steam railways, lovingly cared for by enthusiasts and enjoyed by old and young alike, journey through all parts of the area, offering breathtaking views of the countryside. Throw in exhilarating drives around the Penzance area and on Exmoor and this single colourful and varied volume offers some of the best sights and attractions of one of Britain's most exciting regions. The West Country may not be able to compete with Scotland or Wales in its number of castles, but for some this region will always represent all that is typically English.

✦

Ten generations failed to alter the turn
of a single phrase. In these Wessex nooks the
busy outsider's ancient times are only old; his
old times are still new; his present is futurity

Thomas Hardy (1840–1928), from
'Far From the Madding Crowd'

THE LIZARD
Cornwall

Kynance Cove

'A steep descent leads the traveller to the shore among wild and shaggy rocks where, in the scene which opens before him, he may find the glowing fancies of a fairyland. The rocks appear as if they had been purposely grouped: and by their dark and varied colours pleasingly contrast with the light tints of the sandy beach and azure sea. The predominant colour of the serpentine is an olive green, but it is divided by waving lines of red and purple, while many of the rocks are encrusted by the yellow lichen or seamed by veins of steatite.' Murray's *Handbook for Devon and Cornwall* (1859)

The tip of the Lizard Peninsula, with its guardian lighthouse, is the furthest south you can go in England. Along the coast cliffs rising to 200ft (60m) are broken by little rocky coves, with here and there a tiny fishing village and harbour. The Lizard is known for its unique serpentine rock, predominantly green in colour. Serpentine ornaments became fashionable in Victorian times and are still made here as souvenirs. Soapstone was also extracted here. The church at Landewednack has a pulpit and lectern made of the curious stone. Much of the coast is cared for by the National Trust, including Mullion Cove, with its charming old harbour and island bird sanctuary, and Kynance Cove, a popular beauty spot known for its serpentine cliffs, caves and rock formations, where the sea spouts and hisses through a fissure called the Devil's Bellows. On the eastern side of the peninsula are the simple, white-washed cottages of Cadgwith and Coverack, the latter a celebrated smugglers' haven whose name is Cornish for `hideaway'. Offshore lie the dreaded reefs of the Manacles, which have torn the life out of many a proud ship. Drowned seamen sleep their last sleep in the churchyard at St Keverne, whose tall spire was a vital landmark for ships in the Channel. Cornwall is well-served with tales of mermaids, and a story is told of an old man at Cury, near the Lizard, who rescued a stranded mermaid and put her back in the water. He was granted three wishes, and some years later, it is said, she returned for him, taking him down into the watery depths.

The curve of Lizard Point

Looking north along Kynance Cliffs on the peninsula's western coast

ST MICHAEL'S MOUNT
Cornwall

MOUNTS BAY, ½ MILE (1 KM) OFFSHORE FROM MARAZION

In ancient times St Michael's Mount may well have been the Isle of Ictis, which was known to Greek travellers and merchants. It was for many years an important port, not only for the export of Cornish tin, but also for trade in Irish gold and copper.

Like its counterpart in France, St Michael's Mount is set on an island close to the shore

An old Cornish legend claims that in the 5th century some fishermen saw the Archangel St Michael on a ledge of rock on the western side of the Mount, and it has been called St Michael's Mount ever since. The legend of Jack the Giant-Killer also originated here: the giant Cormoran was said to have built the Mount, from where he waded ashore to steal cows and sheep from the locals. Jack rowed out to the Mount one night and dug a great pit while the giant slept. The next morning Cormoran awoke and set off towards the shore, but fell into the pit – which is still shown to children who visit the Mount.

Legends aside, this great rock is a picturesque sight. Perched upon its summit is a building which has been a church, a priory, a fortress and a private home. It was built in 1135 by the abbot of its namesake, Mont St Michel in Normandy, to whom it had been granted by the Norman Earl

of Cornwall. However, the original building was destroyed by an earthquake in 1275. It was difficult, with their French connection, for the monks of St Michael's Mount to prosper during the intervening years as England was constantly at war with France.

For all its isolation, the Mount was seen as strategically important whenever there was turmoil in the country – the Wars of the Roses, the Prayer Book Rebellion, the Armada and, of course, the Civil War, when it was a Royalist stronghold until surrendered to Parliament in 1646, and subsequently taken over as a garrison.

When the military left, the Mount came into the private ownership of the St Aubyn family, but in the days when travel was arduous and social connections were paramount it left much to be desired. In fact, the Mount remained largely unoccupied, used only occasionally during the summer, until the late 18th century when the family began to look upon the Mount as a more permanent residence. Undaunted by the fact that the living quarters were not of an adequate size, they set about the construction of a great new wing – obviously not an easy task on a great rock which is cut off at every high tide.

The St Aubyns were obviously a force to be reckoned with and the splendid Victorian apartments that they added are as much a testament to their determination as to their good taste. There are some fine plaster reliefs, beautiful Chippendale furniture and collections of armour and pictures.

Open from April to October on weekdays. Tel: 01736 710507.

Manderley and Troy Town
The wealthy merchant dynasty of Rashleigh had their country house outside Fowey at Menabilly. It was later for many years the home of Daphne du Maurier, who dearly loved this part of Cornwall and put it into many of her novels and adventure stories. Menabilly itself is the 'Manderley' of *Rebecca* and also appears in *The King's General*. Another well-known literary figure, Sir Arthur Quiller-Couch (or 'Q'), lived in Fowey for more than 50 years. His house was The Haven on the esplanade and 'Troy Town' was his fictional Fowey

Fowey's lively harbour square

FOWEY
Cornwall

7 MILES (11 KM) SOUTH OF LOSTWITHIEL

The steep, narrow streets of this pleasant old town plunge down the hillside above a lovely, yacht-crowded haven on the estuary of the River Fowey. Blessed with one of the best natural harbours on the south coast, Fowey (the name is pronounced to rhyme with 'toy') was an important port in the Middle Ages, on the trade route between the Continent and Ireland which crossed Cornwall overland to the Camel estuary. Its piratical seamen, the 'Fowey Gallants', were not averse to preying on ships in the English Channel and even raiding the French coast, sometimes provoking fierce retaliation – the French came and burned the town down in 1457. In the 19th century local ships traded to the Mediterranean and across the Atlantic, and Fowey became a china clay port. The parish church of St Fimbarrus has some fine monuments to the Rashleigh family, whose 15th-century town house is now the Ship Inn. The Lugger Inn is a 17th-century hostelry, the town hall in Trafalgar Square – now housing a museum – dates from the 1790s, and there are many other interesting old buildings.

LOOE
Cornwall

7 MILES (11 KM) SOUTH OF LISKEARD

*A*nother old port of character is set on the steep banks of the River Looe (the name rhymes with 'woo'). West Looe and East Looe, facing each other across the harbour and connected by a bridge, were separate towns until the 1880s, and each little place solemnly sent two MPs to Westminster until 1832. Cornish granite was also exported from here, including the stone to build Westminster Bridge and the Embankment in London. Most of West Looe today dates from after the arrival of the railway in 1869. East Looe is the larger and more interesting of the towns, with narrow cobbled streets and twisting alleys. Old buildings go back to the 16th century, including the Fisherman's Arms inn and the Old Guildhall, which is now a museum of local history. A popular resort with a sandy beach, East Looe developed shark fishing as a visitor attraction in the 1950s, and the Shark-sighting Club of Great Britain has its headquarters here. There are boat trips to the bird sanctuary on Looe Island, and inland up the two branches of the river. High on the cliffs to the east is the delightful Monkey Sanctuary, a colony of woolly monkeys from the Amazon rain forests which fraternise amicably with visitors.

Boats and birds bask in Looe harbour sunshine

Launceston Castle was an important military fortress in its time

LAUNCESTON CASTLE
Cornwall

LAUNCESTON, 23 MILES (37 KM) NORTH-WEST OF PLYMOUTH

King Henry III had a younger brother named Richard. It was, perhaps, an unfortunate twist of fate that made Henry the older of the two boys, for Richard was a skilful politician, a cunning diplomat and was wiser by far than his brother the King. Richard used his considerable talents to make himself one of the richest barons in the country – amassing far more wealth than Henry had ever possessed – and with his wealth came a different sort of power. He was elected King of the Romans, and even tried to secure himself the position of Holy Roman Emperor. In 1227, Richard was made Earl of Cornwall, and it was he who built the fine castle at Launceston.

Launceston is a good example of what is known as a shell keep, which consists of a circular wall with buildings inside. Inside this outer wall Richard built another tower, roofed over the space between the two walls, and added a fighting platform around the outside of the outer wall. After Richard's death in 1272, Launceston declined in importance as a military fortress, and by 1353 it was reported that pigs were endangering its foundations by trampling the moat. Launceston was also used as a prison, and it is believed that George Fox, the founder of the Quakers, was held here for eight months in 1656.

Open from Easter to September daily. Tel: 01566 772365.

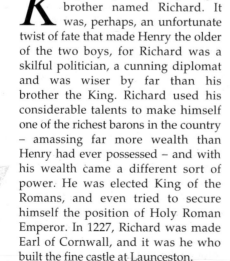

The granite village that seems to grow out of the landscape

ZENNOR
Cornwall

4 MILES (6 KM) SOUTH-WEST OF ST IVES

West Penwith is Celtic Cornwall at its most inspiring, a patch of England on which modern man has left little mark. The weathered, grey buildings of the village of Zennor huddle together in a dip in this ancient granite landscape, lumps of stone strewn around, trees struggling to beat the gales. The church is old but much altered and is chiefly known for the 15th-century bench-end, now part of a chair, on which is carved the famous mermaid of Zennor who, according to legend, lured the squire's son down to her home beneath the waves. The Wayside Museum depicts the industrial past of the area, also reflected in the name of the pub, the Tinners' Arms, where D H Lawrence drank while living near by during World War I, at work on his novel *Women in Love*. To the north-west of the village are the jagged cliffs of Zennor Head and the rugged stretch of coastline on either side. Just inland, up on the bleak, treeless moorland, is Zennor Quoit, a Neolithic chambered tomb with a capstone 18ft (5.5m) long that was supported on five upright stones until vandalised by farmers in the 19th century. One end now rests on the ground. All around, in the bracken and gorse, are field boundary walls that were built by Iron Age Celtic farmers and have stood, timeless, through the centuries.

'A tiny granite village nestling under high shaggy moor-hills, and a big sweep of lovely sea beyond, such a lovely sea, lovelier ever than the Mediterranean…It is all gorse now, flickering with flowers; and then it will be the heather; and then, hundreds of fox gloves. It is the best place I have been in, I think.'
D H Lawrence, writing to J M Murry and Katherine Mansfield from Zennor, March 1916

LANHYDROCK HOUSE
Cornwall

2½ MILES (4 KM) SOUTH-EAST OF BODMIN

*L*anhydrock House could easily have looked very different indeed to the lovely, symmetrical Tudor mansion ranged around three sides of a courtyard that we see today. The fact is that only the north wing, entrance porch and gatehouse are original. The rest of the 17th-century house was destroyed by fire in 1881, at a time when all too often the conservation of the past was sacrificed to Victorian enthusiasms. Fortunately, the owner, Lord Robartes, had the house rebuilt in the exact style of the remaining portion, using the same grey granite and recreating what is one of the most delightful compositions in the country.

Inside, though, it is pure Victoriana and a tour of the house gives a vivid insight into the lives of both the owners and their staff in those times. The 'below stairs' parts of the house are fascinating, and include an enormous kitchen with its larders and a dairy, still with the equipment and utensils required to feed a great household. The tour also includes the bakehouse, cellars and the servants' quarters. Of the grander apartments, the Long Gallery, in the original wing, is particularly splendid. It is 116ft (35m) long and has an intricately carved plasterwork ceiling depicting scenes from the Old Testament, worked by local craftsmen in the mid-17th century. Throughout, the house is furnished in fine style with some lovely 18th-century furniture and tapestries.

The house was given to the National Trust in 1953, having belonged to the Robartes family since 1620 when Sir

Symmetrical wings give Lanhydrock a particular air of formality

Richard Robartes, a Truro banker, bought the estate. In 1624 James I made him a baron, which may have prompted the building of the house. The beginning of construction work certainly coincided with the bestowing of the title. Unfortunately, Sir Richard did not live to see his beautiful home completed and it was left to his son to finish the work.

The gatehouse, another survivor from the original building, now stands alone as the main entrance to the house and the formal Victorian gardens. These cover some 22 acres (9ha) and consist of herbaceous borders and formal parterres, with clipped yews and bronze urns. There are also beautiful rhododendrons, camellias and magnolias. Beyond the gardens, the estate extends to around 1,000 acres (400ha) of meadows and woodland, with a network of footpaths.

Open from April to October daily, except Monday, but open Bank Holiday Mondays. Tel: 01208 73320.

The intricate ceiling of the famous Long Gallery shows Old Testament scenes

TREBAH
Cornwall

MAWNAN SMITH, 3 MILES (5 KM) SOUTH OF FALMOUTH

Even by Cornish standards, the gardens of Trebah are remarkable. Covering 25 acres (10ha), they occupy a ravine some 500yds long which runs from a fine 18th-century house at its head to a private beach on the Helford River, dropping more than 200ft (61m) in the process. Its original creator, Charles Fox, came to Trebah in 1826, and to shelter the ravine from the fierce coastal winds he planted a great screen of maritime pines, *Pinus pinaster*, behind which seeds and plants collected from all over the world could flourish.

A stream runs through a water garden in the upper part of Trebah, created since 1981 by the present owners, Major and Mrs Hibbert, who have also placed the gardens in a charitable Trust to ensure that this extraordinary conception cannot die in the future. Small pools edged with primulas and water irises, astilbes and ligularias, bamboo and ferns give colour and form to the scene, while the lower part of the ravine supports the largest *Gunnera manicata* (Brazilian rhubarb) that most people are ever likely to see.

A dense network of paths leads either down in to the valley, just a short way down to the Koi Pool and waterfall, or along the Camellia Walk to a viewpoint overlooking the beach. Below, many species of rhododendron flower in the spring and early summer. Some, including 'Trebah Gem', which was planted in 1900, have now reached 45ft (13m) in height, while two R. *'Loderi'* 'King George' have delicate pink buds which open in May as large white, fragrant blooms.

Trebah is famous for its tender trees and shrubs. A large Chilean laurel with bright green, aromatic leaves can be seen in the Chilean Combe, and the dogwood, 'Bentham's Cornel', with its yellow bracts, does well. Magnolias, including *Magnolia x soulangiana*, and the pink tulip tree, are also well represented, as are many varieties of eucalyptus, pieris and tree ferns. Three extremely tall Chusan palm trees dominate the view down the ravine, and you can also see a pocket handkerchief tree and an exotic though actually quite hardy Chinese fir. Alas, when temperatures fell to -15°C in January 1987 Trebah lost many beautiful trees, including the largest *Eucalyptus overta* in England and a *Rhododendron sinograndes*, which was thought to be more than a hundred years old.

Special care has been taken to extend the flowering season of the garden right through to Christmas with acres of blue and white hydrangeas.

Open daily throughout the year. Tel: 01326 250448.

Left, the three tall Chusan palms dominate the view down the valley

Below, exotic tree ferns fill the old quarry

TRESCO ABBEY GARDENS
Tresco, Isles of Scilly

A brilliant cluster of South African lampranthus

Few gardens are reached by a more exciting journey than the Abbey Gardens on Tresco, one of the Isles of Scilly. There is a choice of either taking the *Scillonian* from Penzance, and then a launch from St Mary's, or a helicopter – also from Penzance – that goes direct to the garden gates. The gardens represent a remarkable work of construction by their founder, Augustus Smith, in 1834, and they are maintained today by his descendant, the present owner, R A Dorrien Smith.

Tresco lies in the Atlantic 30 miles (48km) off the coast of Cornwall and is warmed by the Gulf Stream. Although the temperatures in winter rarely fall below 10°C, exceptional sub-zero temperatures in January 1987 caused terrible damage to some of the sub-tropical plants. Of course, the wind is an ever-present enemy, and with great forethought, Augustus Smith provided his three great terraces, the Long Walk and the Middle and Top Terraces, with shelter-belts of Monterey cypress, tall hedges of holm oak and high, retaining walls. These also provide an effective setting for the granite house that he built near the ruins of a Benedictine priory.

The 14 acre (5.5ha) gardens are home to many exotic plants, including the South African proteus, the tender geranium from Madeira, *G. maderense*, tall date palms from the Canary Islands and the striking Chilean *Myrtus luma* which has orange-coloured bark. There are also acacias, eucalyptus and the New Zealand *Metrosideros tomentosa* which is 80ft

(24m) tall, has a great number of aerial roots and produces crimson flowers in summer.

Around St Nicholas's Priory honeysuckles, the blue-flowering *Convolvulus mauritanicus* and the pretty Mexican daisy spill out of cracks in the ancient walls and arches, and there is a magnificent rock garden excavated into a 40ft (12m) cliff below. The Middle Terrace has an area known as Mexico, and is covered with the turquoise flowers of *Puya alpestris* from Chile. Further along, a stone summerhouse is overgrown with Burmese honeysuckle.

Tresco Abbey gardens offer many unusual delights, but no visitor should miss the so-called Valhalla. Open on one side, the building houses some of the figureheads of ships that have foundered on the treacherous rocks of the Isles of Scilly during the last three centuries.

Open all year. Tel: 01720 422849.

Above, the exotic flower of a King protea

Left, a different sort of garden ornament – a ship's figurehead from 'Valhalla'

PENZANCE AND LAND'S END

This 46-mile (74km) drive takes you around the western tip of England, an area exposed to the prevailing winds and violent storms and yet warmed by the great Atlantic Ocean. Scattered remains of ancient settlements and abandoned mines add to the mystery of this isolated peninsula.

DIRECTIONS

Leave Penzance by following the signs to Newlyn and Mousehole, beside the harbour. At Newlyn cross the bridge and turn left, unclassified (sp. Mousehole) to reach Mousehole. Turn left down a very narrow lane then turn right alongside the harbour. Turn right into Fore Street (sp. Paul) and continue up a steep hill to Paul. Continue forward to pass the church (sp. Land's End) and in ½ mile turn left on to the B3315 to Sheffield. In a further 5 miles, at the trunk road, turn left, then in ½ mile descend (hairpin bends) to the outskirts of Treen. In 1¼ miles turn right, and 2 miles further turn

left on to the A30 for Land's End. Return along the A30 through Sennen and in 1¼ miles turn left on to the B3306 (sp. St Just). In 3 miles further, at the trunk road, turn left on to the A3071 for St Just. Here, go forward on to the B3306 then descend and follow signs for St Ives to reach Pendeen.

Continue to the edge of Morvah, then at the Gurnards Head Hotel bear right then keep left to pass the outskirts of Zennor. Continue to St Ives. Here, turn right on to the A3074 (sp. Hayle) for Carbis Bay and Lelant. Here, turn right and in ½ mile, at the mini-roundabout, bear right (sp. Penzance). At the next roundabout take 3rd exit, A30 to Canonstown and Crowlas. In a further mile, at the roundabout, take 2nd exit, unclassified (sp. Marazion). In ⅓ mile further turn left to Marazion to view St Michael's Mount. Return, unclassified (sp. Penzance) to Longrock. Here, at the roundabout, join the A30. Go forward at the next roundabout and turn left at the third one to re-enter Penzance.

Little boats shelter in the harbour at Mousehole

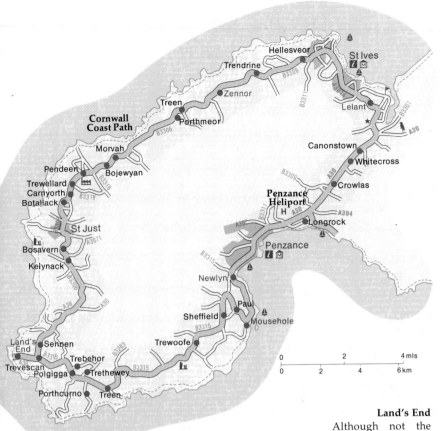

>> ON THE TOUR >>

Penzance

The most westerly town in England, Penzance lies on the north-west corner of Mount's Bay commanding views across the sweeping expanse of water as far as Lizard Point. Away from the quay a network of lanes reveals many fine Regency buildings, especially in Chapel Street. The Nautical Museum contains evidence of the ferocity of the seas along this coast with numerous items discovered from wrecked ships. Further to the west are Morrab Gardens, with a sumptuous display of sub-tropical plants. The Trinity House National Lighthouse Centre is at Penzance Harbour.

Newlyn

Numerous valleys and courtyards crowd round the pretty harbour of this busy fishing village. The beauty of the clear light attracted a group of artists at the beginning of the present century; their work is on permanent display in the Newlyn Art Gallery.

Mousehole

Regarded as the epitomy of the Cornish fishing village, Mousehole, pronounced 'Mowzel', retains its charm and feeling of history in its busy quay and granite houses hugging the hillside. From here, the view across Mount's Bay is unsurpassed.

Land's End

Although not the most spectacular part of Cornwall's coast, Land's End has a unique appeal; seeing the last inn, house and church in England has a satisfaction all of its own. Rocks rise from the sea like giant stepping stones leading the eye to the Longships Lighthouse almost two miles away and, on a clear day, the distant Scilly Isles. A leisure complex displays and interprets the natural history of the area.

St Just

One of the centres of copper mining in Cornwall, there are many industrial remains around St Just, especially near the coast where the shafts run up to half a mile out under the sea. In the town centre is a *plane-an-gwarry*, a circular enclosure where Cornish mystery plays were performed. The church, mostly 15th-century, contains two fine wall paintings and a 5th-century inscribed stone.

Zennor

Isolated for centuries, Zennor has an ancient feel and is surrounded by tiny fields, some of which date back to the Bronze Age. A range of agricultural and mining finds in the area is exhibited in the Wayside Museum, near the car park. The square-towered church has a mermaid carved on one of the bench ends, relating to a legend about a squire's son who had such a fine voice that a mermaid spirited him away to live with her in the sea.

St Ives

Until the early years of this century St Ives was just a fishing port of grey, slate-roofed cottages packed in the lee of a hill overlooking a sheltered harbour. Then, the character of the place and surrounding countryside attracted a bevy of artists – Bernard Leach, Ben Nicholson and Barbara Hepworth amongst them. Barbara Hepworth's home is administered by the Tate Gallery; her studio is intact and the garden planted with sculptures. In summer visitors still flock to the town to enjoy the art galleries and absorb the atmosphere. The beaches south of the town are ideal for families – fine sand gently shelving to the sea.

Lelant

Lying on the Hayle Estuary, the salt flats at Lelant provide the ornithologist with a rich variety of bird life. In the grounds of Quay House is a hide constructed by the RSPB that is open to everyone. In contrast, Merlin's Magic is a theme park with a wide variety of amazing attractions that appeal to children of all ages.

BODMIN & WENFORD RAILWAY
Cornwall

BODMIN, 16 MILES (25 KM) WEST OF LISKEARD

*T*he Bodmin & Wenford Railway offers a unique opportunity to compare the most modern of rail services with the nostalgia of the age of steam. It is the only preserved railway which is served by 125mph (200kph) High Speed Trains, and after being whisked from London Paddington or Edinburgh, passengers can cross a covered footbridge at Bodmin Parkway to an island platform from which Bodmin & Wenford trains depart. The 3½-mile (5.5 km) line, originally opened by the Great Western Railway in 1887, is the only standard gauge preserved railway in Cornwall, and recalls the days when the county was served by a fine network of picturesque branch lines to many of the principal resorts and market towns.

As the branch line turns away from the main line, it crosses a five-arch viaduct across the River Fowey, which rises on Bodmin Moor, then begins a taxing climb through wooded cuttings towards the one intermediate stop at

Passing Charlie's Gate

Colesloggett Halt. This was built by the Bodmin & Wenford to serve a network of paths created by the Forestry Commission through nearby Cardinham Woods. The railway's guide book contains a description and a map of the woods showing the four routes through them; cycles can be hired at the entrance and refreshments are available at an adjacent café.

The climb continues through banks of bracken and foxgloves with fine views northwards over the fields to Bodmin Moor. On the outskirts of Bodmin the railway's largest steam locomotive, Southern Railway West Country class No 34007 *Wadebridge*, may be glimpsed on the east side, undergoing restoration beside the Fitzgerald Lighting factory. A little farther on are the redundant barracks of the Duke of Cornwall's Light Infantry. In 1944 the railway brought Field Marshall Montgomery and General Eisenhower to visit the regiment.

As the train enters the station after the 25-minute slog uphill (it takes only 20 minutes going back), a line swings in from the left. This was a link to Boscarne Junction and Wadebridge, which the Bodmin & Wenford hopes to re-open in order to to relieve local roads of china clay lorries as well as to take passengers to the Camel Trail. The attractive terminus at Bodmin is a 25-minute walk from the start of this popular trail which extends for 15 miles (24km) to the sea at Padstow. Cycles can be hired in Wadebridge, which is linked by bus to Bodmin and Padstow.

Train service: daily from the end of May to the end of September; also open on certain days in winter. Tel: 01208 73666.

Fireman at work on Swiftsure, a 1943 Hunslet

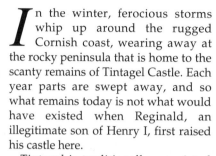

TINTAGEL CASTLE
Cornwall

TINTAGEL, 2 MILES (3 KM) NORTH OF CAMELFORD

*I*n the winter, ferocious storms whip up around the rugged Cornish coast, wearing away at the rocky peninsula that is home to the scanty remains of Tintagel Castle. Each year parts are swept away, and so what remains today is not what would have existed when Reginald, an illegitimate son of Henry I, first raised his castle here.

Tintagel is traditionally associated with the legend of King Arthur, who, it is said, was conceived here while Merlin waited in a cave under the castle. The cave that pierces the thin neck of rock which joins the peninsula to the mainland is still called Merlin's Cave, and it can be visited at low tide. This is a wild and desolate place, where it is easy to imagine the romantic image of the legendary hero, but there is no concrete evidence to support the connection.

About 100 years after Reginald had built his square hall, Richard, Earl of Cornwall, built two more enclosures and raised some walls. The Black Prince built another hall, and there is evidence that yet another was raised over the remains of the previous two. Archaeologically, Tintagel is difficult to understand, and there are foundations of buildings and several tunnels, the purpose of which remains unknown – all adding to the castle's air of mystery.

Open all year, except at Christmas and New Year. Tel: 01840 770328.

Subjected to erosion by the sea, Tintagel Castle is a dramatic sight

PORT ISAAC
Cornwall

Where the stark cliffs of the North Cornwall coast stand guard against the relentless sea between Rumps Point and Tintagel Head, the little harbour of Port Isaac is sheltered by the bulk of Lobber Point. White-washed cottages crowd the narrow streets and lanes, one of which

This Celtic hill fort was excavated in 1904, and pottery from shortly before the Roman period was discovered. The fort has been identified as the Castle Terrible of Thomas Malory's 15th-century epic *Morte D'Arthur* – the spot where Uther Pendragon besieged the Duke of Cornwall.

Stone and iron play harsh tunes at Port Isaac

is so cramped that it is graphically called Squeezebelly Alley. Fishing boats, nets and calling gulls lend atmosphere to a port from which Delabole slate was once shipped, before the railway arrived and took the trade away. Port Isaac was a thriving fishing harbour in the 19th century when the vast shoals of pilchard made their regular appearances along the Cornish coast. They come no more, and the little town depends on visitors for its living today. The handsome old parish church is to the south at St Endellion, and a couple of miles to the east rise the double ramparts (up to 50ft/17m wide) of Tregeare Rounds.

The impressive, romantic castle of Caerhays is set in a famous garden

CAERHAYS CASTLE
Cornwall

GORRAN, 6 MILES (9.5 KM) SOUTH OF ST AUSTELL

Caerhays is a name which was known at the time of the Domesday Book, and though the castle has all the appearance of a great Norman fortress, it is, in fact, a product of the 19th century. It was built for one John Bettesworth Trevanion, who inherited Caerhays in 1801 at the age of 21. It is not clear why Trevanion felt the need for such an impressive new home on land which had been in the family since 1390, nor why he should choose John Nash – very fashionable and very expensive – as his architect. What is known for sure is that the cost of it ruined the family and by 1840 they retreated in debt to Paris, where John died.

The castle then stood empty, rapidly declining, for 13 years until it was bought by Michael Williams, a Cornish Member of Parliament, mine owner and industrialist. He and his son, John, are credited with the restoration of the castle, while the next two generations created and maintained the delightful gardens and grounds which surround it. Now in its fifth generation, the Williams family is still at Caerhays.

Today there are few reminders of the Trevanions, apart from a number of family portraits, and most of the furniture is modern.

Open between March and May on selected days. Tel: 01872 501310.

Houses cluster round the granite harbour

Stargazy Pie

This is a local dish made with whole fish whose heads stick out through the pastry crust. Traditionally, it is eaten here on Tom Bawcock's Eve, 23 December. Tom was a Mousehole fisherman who is said to have saved the villagers from starvation after going out in a storm and bringing back a huge catch of seven different kinds of fish.

MOUSEHOLE
Cornwall

2 MILES (3 KM) SOUTH OF PENZANCE

Phoenician tin merchants came here 2,500 years ago and it is thought the name Mousehole (pronounced 'Mowzel') may derive from their word for watering place. A little more recently, in 1595, the village fell victim to 200 Spaniards who landed here from four galleons, raping the women and burning just about all the houses bar the former manor house in Keigwin Street. Since then the village has rebuilt itself in the narrow streets and alleys that twist uphill from the curving granite quays of the harbour. This was once the centre of Cornwall's pilchard-fishing industry, but the pilchards had left the Cornish waters by the turn of the century and now only a few boats operate from here. Among the grey-brown granite houses, with their lichen-covered slate roofs and splashes of fuschia and hydrangea, stand two large Methodist chapels, a reminder of John Wesley's activities in this area. The village church is some way up the hill, in the parish of Paul. Here may be found a memorial to Dolly Pentreath who died in 1777, allegedly the last person to speak – and swear – solely in Cornish. In 1981 disaster struck the village again when the Penlee lifeboat went down with its entire crew – all Mousehole men.

DARTMOOR

Dartmoor is often dubbed the last wilderness of southern Britain, but wilderness is a relative term and although the 368 square mile (953 sq km) National Park appears at first sight to consist of an open, bleak, moorland core crossed by few roads, everywhere you look reveals evidence of human presence. Nowhere in north-western Europe has a greater density of prehistoric remains, and nowhere in Britain can you feel the same brooding sense of a past extending over 5,000 years.

Previous pages, the granite bastions of Houndtor, Dartmoor National Park

Bronze Age Dartmoor – the remains of a hut circle at Grimspound

Now I am no horseman, so I approached the pony-trekking trip across the heart of Dartmoor with some trepidation. But I needn't have worried. Our mounts were almost boringly docile, and seemed to know every hoofprint of the way between Manaton, on the eastern side of the moor, and our lunch stop at the Warren House Inn, where the roaring open fire in the bar is said to have been kept burning for a hundred years - a testimony to the bleakness of its situation.

We began our excursion by climbing up from the conifer belts of Natsworthy, following the ridge above the East Webburn River between Hameldown Tor and Hookney Tor. The haul had been long and slow, but as we breasted the col between the tors, and the Challacombe valley was revealed below, we looked down on a landscape which was the epitome of Dartmoor. In the foreground, encircled by a heather-covered bank, was Grimspound, perhaps the most complete Bronze Age village site in England. The circular hut sites lined with granite moorstone stood out clearly in the dark, chocolate-brown heather, while on the rugged tors above, cairns and tumuli – marked by Gothic lettering on the map – showed where the chieftains of this long-deserted village were buried perhaps

4,000 years ago. In front of us, on the moorland slopes above the enclosures of the 18th-century Headland Warren Farm, the extensive remains of the East Birch Tor Tin Mine indicated where the miners of the 16th century and earlier had dug for the ore, cutting deep, ravine-like gullies into the moor. Below us, in the valley of the West Webburn, the many parallel ridges showed where the miners had streamed for alluvial tin, in much the same way as gold prospectors panned for gold. A straighter, sharp-sided and more continuous gully running the length of the valley marked the course of a leat, or artificial water channel, which had fed a large waterwheel whose pit was still visible in the valley bottom. This wheel powered the pumping rods which drained the East Birch Tor Tin Mine back in the mid-19th century.

The name Headland Warren is a clue to another medieval occupation on Dartmoor. From those times until as late as the mid-20th century rabbits were bred in artificial warrens for their meat, and Headland Warren was one of the biggest. In other places strange cigar-shaped mounds, easily confused with Bronze Age barrows and known to the archaeologist as pillow mounds, show where artificial burrows were made to encourage the rabbits to breed. Further down the valley, on the slopes of Challacombe Down, the distinct lines of parallel terraces could be made out running north–south across the hillside. These were the remains of medieval strip lynchets, created by the build-up of oxen-ploughed soil against the boundaries of the ancient fields which contoured across the hillside. Narrower corrugations within some of them

A farmstead nestles in the lee of the moor, deep in the heart of Dartmoor

The reconstructed clapper bridge at Postbridge

marked the ridge-and-furrow of further medieval cultivations. With more hut circles further down the West Webburn valley and on Challacombe Down, and the remains of a prehistoric stone row marching up its northern flank through the opencast tin workings, the view was a perfect example of what is known as the Dartmoor palimpsest – layer upon layer of human artefacts fossilised in the modern landscape.

You can expect to see many, if not all, of these features during the course of a typical afternoon's walk on Dartmoor, the prehistoric metropolis of our National Parks, and to find the reason for the amazingly complete preservation of the historic features we must look at Dartmoor's geology.

Dartmoor is the last knuckle in a Cyclopean underground granite fist which extends across the West Country from Land's End through Bodmin Moor. About 280 million years ago molten granite forced its way up through the younger, sedimentary rocks above and cooled slowly to form the rough, grey granite we see in the

tors and boulder-strewn valley slopes today. Most of the prehistoric monuments, from the stone circles to the stone rows and territorial boundaries known as reaves which run ruler-straight for mile after mile across the moor, were built of this enduring stone. Perhaps the most impressive natural landforms on the sweeping, sepia-brown moor where the ever-changing shafts of light constantly open up new vistas are those weird, roughly-weathered tors. The name comes from the Old English *torr*, meaning a high rock, and Dartmoor's tors are probably more famous than their millstone grit counterparts in the Pennines. Perhaps the best-known are the massive Hay Tor, looking like the wrinkled back of a sitting elephant on the eastern side of the moor above Bovey Tracey, and nearby Hound Tor, a wild collection of rocks with the well-preserved remains of a medieval village nestling among the bracken and boulder clitter at its foot. One of the strangest tors is the 20ft (6m) high natural rock sculpture of Bowerman's Nose, on Hayne Down

above Manaton. Some people have whimsically likened this artificial-looking pile of granite building blocks to the cartoon character Andy Capp, while others have sensed a much more primitive, primeval presence.

On the opposite side of the great plateau of the moor, Great Mis Tor, Yes Tor and the 100ft (30m) high, lichen-encrusted pile of Vixen Tor look down on the birthplace of the River Tavy. All the tors are different and highly individual, yet all were formed in the same way. After years of discussion about their origin, most experts now seem to agree that they are the result of high bosses of granite being exposed to the weathering agents of ice, frost, wind and rain for centuries. Eventually the joints were prised open, leaving the upstanding masses of rock we see today.

Combstone Tor, typical of Dartmoor's granite outcrops

Dartmoor obviously takes its name from the fact that it is the birthplace of the great River Dart, and the West and East Dart merge at Dartmeet to flow south then east through the pleasant abbey town of Buckfastleigh, eventually entering the English Channel at the port of Dartmouth. The only Dartmoor rivers to head north to the Bristol Channel are the West and East Okements, which meet at Okehampton on the northern edge of the moor. The natural vegetation cover of the moor after the Ice Age and until man began to clear it in Neolithic times was forest. This has been proved by analysis of the large areas of peat covering the highest points of the moor, where the pollen remains of oak, birch, elm and hazel are common. The only places where the visitor can still experience that primeval wildwood are in precious, protected remnants such as Wistman's Wood, on the slopes of the West Dart near Two Bridges, or Black Tor Beare in the West Okement valley above the Meldon Reservoir.

These are among my favourite places on Dartmoor, where the most

The West Dart River, one of the major rivers in this area, near Hexworthy

fantastically stunted and gnarled pendunculate oaks grow straight from the chaotic boulder clitter. Trees and rocks are festooned with dripping grey-green lichens and ferns, creating an enchanted, fairy-tale landscape. They always remind me of an Arthur Rackham illustration, and if you are there on a misty, autumnal day you wouldn't be the least surprised to see one of Dartmoor's fabled pixies popping up from behind the nearest boulder to pass the time of day.

The wildlife of Dartmoor is strictly limited to those species which can adapt to the harsh and often wet conditions of the moor. With an annual rainfall averaging over 60in (152.5cm), and a high risk of snowfall in the winter because of its 2000ft (610m) altitude, Dartmoor is not always the most hospitable of habitats. One magical feature of Dartmoor, caused by its cold, wet winter climate, is the rare ammil, when every leaf, twig and rock is sheathed in a thin layer of ice. If the wind gets up, you may be treated to the ethereal sound of a thousand icy cymbals gently clashing together.

Most famous of Dartmoor's animals is, of course, the wild-maned Dartmoor pony, chosen as the symbol of the National Park authority. Dartmoor ponies are well-known to picnickers for their roadside scavenging, but the Park authority warns against feeding these semi-wild animals. First mentioned in the will of the Saxon Bishop Aelfwold of Crediton, they are thought to have descended from stock released on the

Enchanted Wistman's Wood, near Two Bridges, a remnant of Dartmoor's wildwood

Buckfast Abbey, rebuilt by Benedictine monks and completed in 1937

moor during the Dark Ages. The best time to see them is during the annual autumnal gatherings, or drifts, when they are rounded up and branded.

The mewing cry of the buzzard or the harsh bark of the raven are often the only signs of birdlife on moorland rambles, while the birdlife in the well-wooded valleys, or coombes, which surround the moor is much richer. Here you can expect to see in summer such species as pied flycatcher, wood warbler and redstart, and from the animal world, the occasional roe deer, badger, fox, and even, if you are extremely lucky, an otter. Some of these wild, woodland animals were

undoubtedly among the prey of the first hunter-gatherers who moved in from the coast and first started the clearance of the forested moor. We have already seen how, in prehistoric times, the moor was much more heavily populated than it is today. At least 5,000 hut circles, mainly dating from the Bronze Age, have so far been indentified on the moor, and more evidence of a large and settled resident population is found each year.

A deterioration in the climate from 1000 to 500BC saw the gradual depopulation of the high moor, and the only surviving evidence from the Dark Ages seems to be a ring of Iron

Age hillforts encircling the western approaches of the moor. The settlement pattern which now exists on Dartmoor largely stems from the Saxon and medieval periods when the mineral wealth of the moor, and in particular the discovery of tin ore, or cassiterite, caused another period of intense human activity. Almost everywhere you look on the moor there are the remains of this industrial boom, from the streamworks mentioned previously to the isolated tinners' huts at the heart of the moor.

The tin workers were governed by the so-called Stannary Court, which administered a harsh justice on wrong-doers.The stannary towns, where the ore was assayed, bought and sold, included Ashburton and Chagford within the Park. Lydford was the administrative centre, where the laws were enforced and the luckier offenders finished up in the stern, square-walled Lydford Castle after the application of so-called 'Lydford Law'. Dreaded by generations of Dartmoor people, it is recalled in the doggerel verse:

'First hang and draw
Then hear the cause, is Lydford Law.'

The wealth won from tin, and later copper, silver, lead, and most recently the enormous china clay quarries at Lee Moor at the south-western corner of the Park, brought prosperity to the

A Dartmoor pony grazes peacefully on the open moor above Tavistock

moor dwellers. This is reflected in the fine granite-towered churches at places like Widecombe-in-the-Moor, Lydford and Moretonhampstead, and the lovely old traditional Dartmoor longhouse farmsteads typically found with a thatched, two-storey porch, like that at Lower Tor, near Poundsgate. Dartmoor's hard-wearing granite was also in demand further afield. The moorland quarries at Haytor, for example, provided stone for Nelson's Column, London Bridge, the Holborn Viaduct and New Scotland Yard in the capital. You can still see in the velvety, sheep-cropped grass the stone sets of the earliest horse-drawn tramway which took the stone down to Teignmouth for shipping.

Dartmoor's most notorious building, however, is the grim prison at Princetown, at the very heart of the moor. First constructed in 1806 for French and American prisoners of war, it became a criminal prison in 1850 and has remained so ever since.

Visitors started to come to Dartmoor and appreciate its wild, untamed beauty when the railway reached Exeter in 1844. Guides like James Perrott of Chagford led these early tourists out on to the moor and it was he who, in 1854, originated the custom of the Dartmoor letter boxes by leaving the tourists' visiting cards in a box at remote Cranmere Pool. Now there are about 500 such letter boxes scattered about the moor.

The Dartmoor National Park, set up in 1951, currently receives about eight million visits a year, and it has done a great deal towards improving visitor management and easing life for the 29,100 resident population by its system of special signposting of routes on the narrow, high-hedged lanes, and negotiating management agreements with farmers in ecologically important areas. About 40 per cent of the Park is common land, in which commoners have rights to graze under the Dartmoor Commons Act. Under the provisions of the Act, the Park authority now has joint responsibility for the commons, and public access is assured. Not so in the 15 per cent of the Park's area used by the Ministry of Defence. This is mainly in the northern

Terraced cottages at Ashburton, a convenient centre on the eastern edge of the moor

part of the moor and includes High Willhays (2,038ft/621m) and Yes Tor (2,030ft/618m), which form part of the huge Okehampton and Willsworthy Training Areas. The military has been training on Dartmoor since 1873, but conservationists were dismayed when, in 1991, the Duchy of Cornwall allowed the Army a further 21-year lease on its training area in the heart of the Park, despite the fact that such use is clearly incompatible with National Park purposes. The battle for Dartmoor's conservation is still not won.

The pinnacled tower of St Pancras, Widecombe-in-the-Moor, often known as 'the cathedral of the Moor'

PLYMOUTH
Devon

43 MILES (69 KM) SOUTH-WEST OF EXETER

Plymouth and the Wooden Walls

'The harbour, full of three-deckers, presents a glorious sight; which an Englishman cannot look at without feeling that inward glorying and exultation of mind, which Longinus describes as the effect of the sublime.'
Henry Matthews, *The Diary of an Invalid* (1820)

Busy today with warships, cross-Channel ferries, cargo boats, fishing smacks, yachts and assorted small craft, Plymouth Sound is a magnificent natural harbour of some 4500 acres (1800ha) in extent, formed by the junction of the rivers Tamar and Plym. An inlet on the north-east, Sutton Harbour, was the original port and the Royal Citadel (English Heritage), a fortress with walls up to 70ft (23m) high, was built to protect it in the 1660s. The Royal Naval Dockyard in the Hamoaze (the Tamar estuary) was opened in 1691. Since the 1840s it has all been protected by a colossal mile-long breakwater in the middle of the Sound, designed by John Rennie. Plymouth is one of Britain's great seafaring towns, with a history of maritime enterprise and adventure going far back into the Middle Ages. Armies were shipped over to France from here in the 14th and 15th centuries. The formidable Elizabethan seadogs – Drake, Hawkins,

Smeaton's Tower dominates Plymouth Hoe

Frobisher, Gilbert and Raleigh – all set out from Plymouth on their ventures. Sir Francis Drake sailed from here in 1577 to voyage round the world and in 1588, after calmly finishing his game of bowls on the Hoe, he sailed out of the Sound to give the Spanish Armada a drubbing. Captain Cook set off from Plymouth in the *Resolution* in 1772, to sail round the world. Targeted as a major naval base, the centre of Plymouth was heavily bombed and severely damaged in World War II, and was rebuilt during a period of singularly undistinguished architecture. The narrow streets of the Barbican area close to Sutton Harbour, however, with the fish quay and a bustling market, have retained their old character and atmosphere, and several of the merchants' and ship captains' houses of Tudor times are open to the public. The Mayflower Stone and steps here commemorate the Pilgrim Fathers, who left Plymouth for the New World in the *Mayflower*, in 1620. Overlooking the Sound from the grassy expanse of the Hoe is Smeaton's Tower, the red-and-white striped upper part of the old Eddystone lighthouse. There is a fine aquarium near by, and the City Art Gallery has a good collection of paintings by Sir Joshua Reynolds, who came from Plympton. Plymouth Dome is a 'time travel experience', with the latest technology. No visit should omit a boat trip to see the naval dockyard, and to admire the stupendous ironwork of the Royal Albert Bridge, carrying the railway line across the Tamar, with its simple, proud inscription: 'Isambard Kingdom Brunel, Engineer, 1859'.

SLAPTON SANDS
Devon

5 MILES (8 KM) SOUTH-WEST OF DARTMOUTH

Looking towards Start Point, with the sea on one side of the bar and the Ley on the other

The sea has piled up a long, straight bar of shingle that stretches north for five or six miles up the coast north of Start Point. The A379 road from Kingsbridge to Dartmouth runs along the shore over Slapton Sands – which are actually shingle, though there is sand here at low tide. On the beach grow such plants as sea radish and shore dock, and a monument recalls that this part of the South Hams area of South Devon was taken over as a rehearsal ground for American troops for the D-Day landings in 1944. Several villages were temporarily evacuated so that the soldiers could train for the Normandy beaches, and the monument was presented by the United States Army as a tribute to the local people. Behind and sheltered by the shingle ridge is the freshwater lagoon of Slapton Ley, a mile or so long, up to 10ft (3m) deep and covering about 270 acres (110ha). A nature reserve, it is rich in fish and plant life. The northern end is thick with reeds and willow. Great crested grebe, stonechat, goldcrest, coot and mallard breed here, migrant birds rest here in spring and autumn, and in winter huge flocks of gulls gather on the beach and the Ley.

BRIXHAM
Devon

5 MILES (8 KM) SOUTH OF TORQUAY

William of Orange on the waterfront, with the Golden Hind behind

*T*orbay or 'the English Riviera' is one of the West Country's leading tourist honeypots. At the southern end of the bay, the picturesque harbour and the steep, narrow streets of Brixham lie sheltered in the lee of Berry Head. In 1850 the town claimed to be England's leading fishing port, with more than 270 vessels – brigs, schooners and smacks – amounting to 20,000 tons of shipping. The town still has a fishing fleet, but a much smaller one. At the harbour's edge a statue of William of Orange commemorates his arrival here in 1688 on his way to be proclaimed King William III at Newton Abbot – and later in London. Nearby, a full-size replica of Sir Francis Drake's *Golden Hind*, the ship in which he sailed round the world, is moored close to the old market house. The local history is expounded in Brixham Museum, which has a special section on the coastguard service. Rev Henry Francis Lyte, who took charge of All Saints church in 1824, wrote the familiar hymn 'Abide With Me' in Brixham. A monument in the church-yard recalls 100 sailors who drowned in a terrible storm in 1866, when many boats were driven onto the rocks. The town's more modern Roman Catholic church has the curious and possibly unique distinction of having a carpark located on its roof.

Keeping It on Ice

The Great Western Railway arrived in Brixham in 1868, and gave the local fishing industry an instant boost by putting the harbour only seven hours away from London. The industry flourished on into the 20th century, but by 1939 a mere half dozen boats were left of Brixham's once proud fishing fleet. Something of a revival came in the 1960s, however, and a new fish market and deep water jetty, with its own ice-making plant, were opened in 1971.

*The pump at the southern
end of Fore Street, installed
for the use of farmers at
the market*

※
CHULMLEIGH
Devon

15 MILES (24 KM) SOUTH-EAST OF BARNSTAPLE

※

The Barnstaple Inn, a thatched, granite building on the northern fringes, is dated 1633 but may be of earlier origin. At that time it was a local court-house and had a gibbet over the door for the immediate execution of convicted

Chulmleigh is a good example of how changing transportation systems can affect fortune's ebb and flow. The village grew up at the junction of five ancient roads and developed as an important market centre in what was, even before *Domesday*, a prosperous sheep-farming area. Its 15th-century church is a proud reminder of those days, its granite tower visible for miles around. Inside is an excellent, wide rood screen and a wagon roof with good bosses and ribs supported by the outspread wings of 38 carved angels. The market was held in Fore Street, where its old pump still stands. The King's Arms, with its grand façade, was a busy coaching inn with extensive stabling

for the horses. In 1830, however, a new turnpike from Exeter to Barnstaple bypassed the town (meaning loss of trade for the King's Arms of course) and in 1854 the railway came and markets moved to stations. Even before then, competition from the North had dealt a blow to the woollen trade, and soon improvements in farming practices led to further unemployment. Add to this two disastrous fires in the 19th century, and Chulmleigh's days of prosperity were numbered. Some wonderful old merchants' houses, many cob, stone and thatched cottages, as well as a medieval toll-house, have survived, however, and Chulmleigh today is a fascinating place to explore.

CLOVELLY
Devon

10 MILES (16 KM) WEST OF BIDEFORD

Clovelly is one of England's show-places, and has been since Kingsley and Dickens drew attention to it in the 19th century. That it remains both well-preserved and remarkably unspoilt is due largely to the lords of the manor, the Hamlyns. In particular, Christine Hamlyn, whose initials can be seen on many of the houses, kept the motor car away and to this day all vehicles have to be left at the top of the village. Sledges are used to carry provisions down the one very steep, cobbled street that leads down 400ft (122m) to the pretty harbour, built when fishing first became profitable in the 16th century.

So steep and narrow is the High Street (called Up-along or Down-along, according to which way you are going) that the little whitewashed houses spill down on both sides in a great jumble, one on top of the other. Its setting in a thickly wooded cleft is best appreciated from the pier. These woods, as well as the 3 mile (4.8km) Hobby Drive, were planted by an early 19th-century Hamlyn. In the church, half a mile above and away from the village, are monuments to earlier lords of the manor, the Careys, as well as Hamlyns, and one to Charles Kingsley, whose *Westward Ho!* and *The Water Babies* were written here.

*Three fishers went sailing
  away to the west,
Away to the west as the sun
  went down;
Each thought on the woman
  who loved him the best,
And the children stood
  watching them out of the
  town.*

Charles Kingsley, 'The Three Fishers'

Up-along…or Down-along

The house remains an intriguing record of two remarkable Victorian architects

KNIGHTSHAYES COURT
Devon

BOLHAM, 2 MILES (3 KM) NORTH OF TIVERTON

Though principally famous for its wonderful gardens, Knightshayes Court is well worth a visit in its own right. Its foundation stone was laid in 1869 but it took so long for work to progress that the architect, William Burges, was sacked in 1874 and J D Crace was appointed to complete the decoration. His painted ceilings and wall stencilling, hidden by later decorations, are being uncovered and restored.

Many of the features installed by Burges also remain, including some delightfully whimsical corbel figures, wood panelling, a great painted bookcase in the stairwell and a series of architectural drawings. In fact, many of the rooms at Knightshayes are an amalgam of the styles of Burges and Crace, endowing them with a unique interest.

The house was built for John Heathcoat-Amory, MP for Tiverton, and remained in the family until the 3rd Baronet, Sir John, died in 1972, leaving the property to the National Trust. The house still contains much of the family furniture and china, together with a collection of Old Masters and some fine family portraits.

Of particular interest is the Golf Room, which illustrates Lady Heathcoat-Amory's golfing career. As Miss Joyce Wethered, she was four-times winner of the Ladies Open in the 1920s.

Open April to October on selected afternoons. Tel: 01884 254665/257381.

HEMERDON HOUSE
Devon

2 MILES (3.5 KM) NORTH-EAST OF PLYMPTON

Curiously, the man who built Hemerdon House had a father and father-in-law who shared the same name (Thomas Woollcombe) and the same occupation (surgeons) in the same town (Plymouth). The two were, in fact, related and young George and his wife Maria were cousins. It was Maria who brought the estate into the marriage and the house they built there was begun in 1793.

Delightfully unpretentious, the Georgian house is particularly interesting for the documentation of its occupation kept by successive generations of Woollcombes. Other mementoes of members of the family include the naval uniform and sword of George, son of the original owners, who rose to the rank of Vice Admiral and was wounded at the Battle of New Orleans. His brother, William, fought at Waterloo.

The present owner of Hemerdon, James Woollcombe, has undertaken much restoration in recent years, including the repairing and rebinding of the excellent collection of books in the library, which date from 1546 to the present. Works of art around the house include two portraits by Reynolds, others by Opie and Gand, and some local landscapes.

Open for 30 days between May and September. Tel: 01752 841410.

A pleasing jumble of family photographs and other treasures adorns the piano

THE GARDEN HOUSE
Devon

BUCKLAND MONACHORUM, 5 MILES (8 KM) SOUTH OF TAVISTOCK

Above, the captivating walled garden with its deep borders

Right above, a carved stone doorway leading to the Garden House

Right below, an example of the delicate Campanula lactiflora

Situated on a hillside to the west of Dartmoor, the Garden House covers 7 acres (2.8ha) of a valley which runs down to the River Tavy. There are records of a vicarage at Buckland Monachorum in the 14th century, but the old tower with its spiral staircase, which is such a feature of the walled garden, dates from the 16th century when the abbot of the dissolved Buckland Abbey changed his religious affiliations to become the vicar. After 1945 the garden was the creation of Lionel Fortescue, a retired Eton classics master, and his wife, but today the garden is owned by a trust, and the planting is in the hands of Keith and Ros Wiley who have gardened at Buckland since 1978.

As you enter the walled garden from the plant sales centre, the impact of the long, grassed path flanked by deep, colourful borders is quite captivating. Astilbes, campanulas, lilies and the gentle pink of *Lavatera* 'Barnsley' are planted among old roses, including 'Golden Wings' and 'Dortmund'. At this lower level the soil is damp and hostas and the rheums flourish, while erythroniums, wood anemones and crocuses flower in the spring. A short flight of steps takes you down into a little dell where magnolias, roses and philadelphus add their distinctive scents.

Throughout the garden care has been taken to group trees and shrubs for the harmony and the contrast of

their foliage and flowers, so the red and the paler berberis can be seen, as can the purple of cotinus and the silver of willows and dogwoods, particularly the *Cornus controversa* 'Variegata', the 'wedding cake tree', with its white, star-shaped flowers. The exacting standards in colour harmony set by the garden's creators have been maintained today, so that a deep blue clematis is partnered by *Viburnum tomentosum*, with its lace-cap flowers and red fruits.

The tower staircase provides access to the second terrace. Here is the main lawn with a round stone seat formed like a lookout at the far end, its entrance guarded by two willows underplanted with cranesbill. There is also an alpine garden where miniature geraniums grow alongside silver plants, and on the very top terrace is a fine collection of rhododendrons, a willow-leaved magnolia, and a *Magnolia x loebneri* 'Leonard Messel', which has lilac-pink petals in mid-spring. This is a delightful place with rare plants – many of which can be bought in the nursery – that never loses the intimacy and individuality of a private garden.

Open daily, from April to September. Tel: 01822 254769.

POWDERHAM CASTLE
Devon

POWDERHAM, 6 MILES (9.7 KM) SOUTH OF EXETER

One of the oldest living creatures in the world resides at Powderham Castle. Timothy, the Mediterranean spur-thighed tortoise, is 155 years old and happily inhabits the rose garden at the foot of the east tower. From here he can survey the gardens, parkland and the River Exe.

Powderham Castle, considerably older than it looks, has belonged to the Courtenay family, Earls of Devon, for some 600 years. Most of the alterations and additions to the original house date from the 18th and 19th centuries and it is the elegance of that era which Powderham reflects today.

Originating in France, the Courtenays were related by marriage to the royal house of Valois, and the founder of this line came to Britain with Eleanor of Aquitaine. Later Courtenays have included an Archbishop of Canterbury, a founder Knight of the Garter and even an Heir Presumptive to the throne of England. And yet, if you ask today about famous members of the family, they are just as likely to mention their beloved elderly tortoise as any of these illustrious ancestors! There are many family portraits around the house, including a rather crowded painting of the 2nd Viscount, his wife and their family of 13 daughters and one son. It was the son, the 3rd Viscount, who was instrumental in reviving the Earldom of Devon which had been in abeyance since 1556.

Their Devon home reflects both the passage of time and the changing fortunes of the family from its 14th-century origins through the destruction and rebuilding of the Civil War period to the age of Victorian grandeur. The dining hall, though the most recent addition, is where the family history can be explored through a series of coats of arms going back to about AD1000. The Marble Hall is particularly interesting – it forms the lower half of the medieval Great Hall and still contains the three original arches, though they were plastered at a later date. This room would once have been as high as the staircase hall, with its fine mahogany staircase adorned with carved heraldic beasts and lavish plasterwork; it was completed in 1755 at a cost of £355.14s.0d.

Upstairs, the solar, once the family room of the medieval castle, has a charming collection of toys including a model Tudor house which was made by a retired estate worker. The rest of the house is an enchanting mixture of original medieval features, family portraits, splendid 18th-century decoration and little curiosities such as the narwhal's horn in the first library (listed in old inventories as a unicorn's horn), and the peacock ornament from the Empress of China's sedan chair at the top of the grand staircase.

Open end-March to end-October, except Saturdays. Tel: 01626 890243.

Left, the elegant, high-ceilinged music room, and below, the painted stairwell

COCKINGTON
Devon

1 ½ MILES (2.5 KM) WEST OF TORQUAY

*I*t is not often one can say that a village's recent history may be as significant as its past. During World War II the Prudential Building Society evacuated its staff to Torquay, and a rapport built up with the locals so that, when the privately owned Cockington Estate was about to be split up, the Prudential decided to invest in its thatched cottages and shops en bloc, maintaining them in traditional style and thus preserving on the outskirts of Torquay this quaint Domesday village. Some of the cottages have Saxon origins and the 13th- and 14th-century red sandstone church has Norman foundations. The old forge dates from the 14th century. The only modern building is the thatched Drum Inn,

Horse-drawn carriages bring visitors to this 'olde-worlde' village and its country park

built harmoniously by Sir Edwin Lutyens in 1934. Cockington Court, the Elizabethan manor of the Carys and then of the Mallocks who added its façade, is owned by Torbay Borough Council and is now home to the Devon Rural Skills Trust who provide workspace for such threatened craftsworkers as the blacksmith, hurdlemaker and thatcher. Its grounds are a designated country park, open to all. For decades now horse-drawn carriages have brought visitors out here from Torquay seafront. These visitors have inevitably brought with them such accoutrements of tourism as litter bins and public conveniences, but the village's immediate environment is assured development in a natural and harmonious way.

Dating from the 14th century, Dartmouth Castle was one of the first to be designed for artillery

DARTMOUTH CASTLE
Devon

DARTMOUTH, 13 MILES (21 KM) SOUTH OF TORQUAY

At the mouth of the River Dart a rocky promontory juts out towards the sea, and on this rock stands Dartmouth Castle – an intriguing collection of military buildings spanning six centuries. The most recent addition is a brick gun-shelter built during World War II in anticipation of a German invasion.

A castle was built at Dartmouth in the 14th century, although it was not until the 15th century that the citizens of Dartmouth really began to build their fortress in earnest. It comprised a square tower and a round tower, side by side, moulded to suit the shape of the rock, and is the earliest surviving English coastal castle designed specially for artillery. At the same time, another castle was built opposite Dartmouth at Kingswear, ensuring that no French pirates would be able to penetrate up river to pillage the wealthy town.

The castle itself saw action in the Civil War, when the town was attacked by Cromwell's forces under Sir Thomas Fairfax. In a blaze of gunfire, Fairfax's men stormed the town, taking it within hours and with remarkably few casualties. The 500 Royalists, who had captured Dartmouth Castle after a siege three years before, surrendered their arms on the following day.

Open daily all year, except 24–26 December and 1 January. Tel: 01803 833588.

With its many tourist attractions, Buckfastleigh station (above and opposite) is the line's most popular starting point

SOUTH DEVON RAILWAY
Devon

BUCKFASTLEIGH, 11 MILES (17.5 KM) WEST OF PAIGNTON

Originally known as the Dart Valley Railway, this line is seldom out of view of the River Dart during the 25-minute journey. It is one of the prettiest stretches of the river valley and can be appreciated to the full only from the train, since few roads thread the valley and glimpses of the river are rare. The water is home to salmon and trout, so the lucky passenger might catch sight of a salmon leaping its way up-river to spawn. Flying over the water you may see ducks, swans, herons or even a kingfisher, and beside the line is a profusion of primroses and wild daffodils in spring. If time permits, alight at the lovely intermediate station at Staverton, star of many a film. From here, as from Totnes station, there are pleasant walks to be enjoyed along the river.

In common with other tourist railways in the West Country, the South Devon Railway relies upon holidaymakers for most of its traffic, but no other line began its second life in the way that this one did. The Dart Valley Railway was set up by a group of businessmen who believed that the former Great Western Railway branch line from Totnes to Ashburton could be run as a commercial enterprise, and that a volunteer workforce would not be crucial to its operation. However, a vital section of the line north of the intermediate station at Buckfastleigh disappeared for ever under the new A38 trunk road, restricting re-opening in 1969 to the southern 7 miles (11km). The company soon acquired the Paignton & Dartmouth Railway, which became its principal interest, and today the South Devon Railway is leased from them by new operators who do rely on volunteer labour.

Most passengers join the trains at the Buckfastleigh end of the line, which is easy to reach from the A38, has a large car park and is handy for a number of other tourist attractions. But Totnes has much to recommend it too, and visitors without a car can easily get to the terminus here by public transport – a

new footbridge was opened in 1993 linking Littlehempston (Totnes) station with the town centre and main line station.

Train service: from June to the end of September, Wednesdays and most weekends in April, May and October. Santa specials. Tel: 01364 642338.

EXMOOR

Exmoor's most famous author, R D Blackmore, knew his home-
land well and his descriptive phrase 'the land lies softly', is an
accurate one. This is a gentle, pastoral landscape of rolling moorland, deeply wooded valleys and rich farmland edged by tall
hedges of stunted beech. Where the land meets the sea, however,
Exmoor has a different face. Here, along the 30-mile (48km) stretch
of switchback coastline between Combe Martin and Minehead, is
some of the most spectacular and beautiful coastal scenery in
Britain, and it forms a dramatic highlight to one of the smallest
and most threatened of our National Parks.

Previous pages, the view from the roof of Exmoor, near the summit of Dunkery Beacon

The heather and gorse clad Brendon Hills form an eastern outlier of Exmoor

Exmoor has always attracted writers and artists, from Richard Doddridge Blackmore, author of the Victorian best-seller *Lorna Doone*, to Henry Williamson, whose natural history classic *Tarka the Otter* perhaps captures the essence of Exmoor better than anything which has been written before or since. Williamson wrote his famous tale of Tarka and White-Tip while living in a remote, 1s 6d-(7 ½ p)-a-week, cob-built cottage on the North Devon coast, and his description of the area from the book still takes some beating:

Exmoor is the high country of the winds, which are to the falcons and the hawks; clothed by whortleberry bushes and lichens and ferns and mossed trees in the goyals, which are to the foxes, the badgers, and the red deer; served by rain clouds and drained by rock-littered streams, which are to the otters.

The symbol of the Exmoor National Park authority, set up in 1954 to administer 268 square miles (694 sq km) of beautiful borderland between Devon and Somerset, is the majestic head of a ten-pointer red deer stag. This is Britain's largest animal and, outside Scotland, Exmoor has the largest wild herd. They are direct descendants of the wild deer which roamed the Exmoor forests in prehistoric times.

But Exmoor's red deer are also a major cause of controversy, with opinions deeply split between supporters of the traditional deer hunts, such as those carried out by the famous 'D and S,' the Devon and Somerset Staghounds which have a history going back to Saxon times, and those who find the whole idea of hunting barbaric. One thing is certain, the deer have to be culled to maintain a vigorous herd and the hunting, which has the support of most local farmers and their families, is carried out selectively and is largely sensitive to the deer's life-cycle. There is, for example, no hunting in the late spring and early summer when the calves, brilliantly camouflaged with their dappled coats that look like sunlight shining on dead leaves, are born.

Next to the red deer, Exmoor's most famous native residents are the hardy, shaggy-coated Exmoor ponies – a truly wild rare breed thought to be descended from the indigenous horses which survived the last Ice Age. These sturdy, agile creatures, not much bigger than a Shetland pony, have roamed Exmoor's moors and pastures for thousands of years and their wild, independent nature somehow encapsulates the spirit of Exmoor.

A simple memorial to R D Blackmore stands by the edge of Badgworthy Water, in the heart of Doone country

Where Exmoor
Meets the Sea

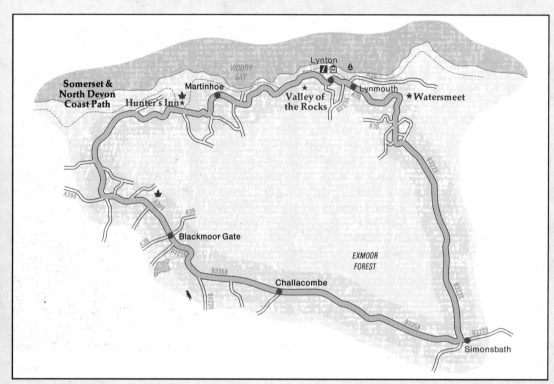

This country drive, of about 31 miles (50km) explores the county boundary between Devon and Somerset, where Exmoor meets the sea. Steep, wooded combes plunge from the high plateau, creating shaded bays strewn with boulders. The scenery is spectacular, both along the coast and inland.

DIRECTIONS

Leave Lynton on the Lynmouth road and, on the descent, turn sharp left on to the B3234. Descend Lynmouth Hill (1 in 4) to Lynmouth. Here, turn right on to the A39 (sp. Barnstable) then reach Watersmeet. In ⅔ of a mile turn left on to the B3223 (sp. Simonsbath) and cross the river bridge. In ¾ mile, at the top of the ascent, turn sharp right to Simonsbath.

Here, turn right on to the B3358 (sp. Blackmoor Gate, Ilfracombe) for Challacombe. In 2⅓ miles, at the trunk road, turn right on to the A399 to Blackmoor Gate. Continue straight ahead on the A399 (sp. Combe Martin), then in 2 miles further, turn right, unclassified (sp. Trentishoe, Hunter's Inn). After 1¼ miles turn right, pass Holdstone car park on the left and in a further mile bear right (sp. Hunter's Inn).

At the Hunter's Inn turn left and ascend (sp. Martinhoe). In ¾ mile, at the top, turn left (sp. Woody Bay, Martinhoe). Pass Martinhoe church and in ½ mile branch left (sp. Woody Bay) then turn left and descend. Continue with signs Lynton, via Toll Road, past the Woody Bay Hotel. Go forward with the narrow coast road and in 1¾ miles, pass through the toll gate. In another mile, at the roundabout, go forward through the Valley of the Rocks and re-enter Lynton.

ON THE TOUR

Lynton

Set high on the cliff-top some 600 feet (200m) above Lynmouth, Lynton became a fashionable resort at the time of the Napoleonic Wars. It abounds in Victorian and Edwardian architecture, epitomised by the splendid town hall, built by the publisher George Newnes, who also sponsored the unusual water-powered cliff railway. The museum in St Vincent's Cottage, crammed with local interest, reflects the activities of the community. From the churchyard an orientation table identifies features on the Welsh coast. The church contains some exceptional marbles, but has been subjected to drab Victorian 'restoration'.

Lynmouth

The Victorians developed Lynmouth from a fishing village, building secluded gabled hotels and villas on the verdant hillsides, and eccentricities like the Rhenish Tower, on the quay, built to store saline bath water. Ferocious floods devastated the village in 1952; 90 houses were destroyed as the River Lyn burst its banks and swept through the sleeping village. Thirty-four people died, and a poignant exhibition records the fateful events in the Flood Memorial Hall.

The oldest area, around Mars Hill, is a medley of colour-washed cottages, and it was here that R D Blackmore stayed whilst researching *Lorna Doone*. Over the little footbridge, the pleasure gardens below the rising mass of Countisbury Hill afford a pleasant picnic area, with children's playground, bowls and a delightful grassy sward adjacent to the shingle beach.

Watersmeet

This aptly named National Trust beauty spot is located where the East Lyn River converges with Hoaroak Water, and cascades down a rocky ravine in a series of waterfalls. Watersmeet House, a fishing lodge built in 1832, offers refreshments during the summer.

Simonsbath

Note the beech hedges and herringbone walls established by John Knight in the 1820s. Access from the car park (signposted from the road) leads to a pleasantly landscaped picnic site, with local tourist information.

The famous water powered cliff railway at Lynton

Hunter's Inn

At Hunter's Inn, set in mature woodland, a path continues to Heddon's Mouth, where the river rushes over smooth pebbles to the sea. For the energetic there is a climb to Heddon's Mouth Cleave, which leaves the path on the west of the river about halfway down. Relax with refreshments at Hunter's Inn afterwards – delightful gardens with ponds and greedy ducks.

Valley of the Rocks

Precarious rock formations pierce the skyline, and top the steep heather-clad hillocks standing sentinel between the sea and the moor; described by poet Robert Southey as 'rock reeling upon rock, stone piled upon stone, a huge terrifying reeling mass.'

A cynical commentator once dubbed Exmoor as 'ex-moor', and the truth is there is not much left of the original 'mountenous and cold ground much be Clouded with thick Foggs and Mists...overgrown with heath, and yielding but a pore kind of turf' which the Parliamentary Commissioners found in 1651. The 'Foggs and Mists' still regularly roll in from the Bristol Channel over the high points of The Chains and Dunkery Beacon, but piecemeal agricultural reclamation has reduced the 'hills of great height covered with heather' noted by Richard Jefferies in 1883, in the moorland heart of the National Park, so that they now cover about a quarter of the total area of the Park as opposed to a third. With luck, the greater power now available to the National Park authority under the Wildlife and Countryside Act of 1981 has stopped the worst of this attrition, although management agreements are still voluntary, and the Park authority has meagre resources with which to buy off the would-be 'improver'.

Having said that, the idea of making the landscape of Exmoor more productive in agricultural terms goes back to 1818 when a Midland ironmaster, John Knight, successfully bid for 15,000 acres (6075ha) of the former Royal Forest of Exmoor. Until then it had been used solely for hunting, with the exception of one not entirely successful attempt to grow oak trees to provide timber for the Navy.

During the next few decades John Knight and his son Frederic transformed the face of Exmoor by draining the waterlogged peats of the high ground, creating new farms and establishing the 'capital' of the forest at Simonsbath, and building the characteristic, beech-topped, earthen-banked hedges – such as the 29 mile (47km) example encircling Forest Wall – which are such a distinctive hallmark of Exmoor. John Knight's dream of growing arable crops on the heights, where the rainfall can be up to 60ins (152cm) a year, was never practical, but Frederic's system of root crop and grassland rotation is operated by some Exmoor farmers to this day. Knight also created one of the few stretches of open water in the National Park when he employed 200 Irish labourers in 1830 to build a dam across the headwaters of the River Barle, just beneath the boggy heights of The Chains near Challacombe. The result,

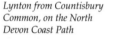

Lynton from Countisbury Common, on the North Devon Coast Path

Pinkworthy (pronounced Pinkery) Pond, is one of Exmoor's special wild places, now in the safe ownership of the National Park authority. Wimbleball Reservoir, a 370 acre (150ha) artificial lake created by the flooding of the Haddeo valley some 5 miles east of Dulverton, is of much more recent construction, but nevertheless very popular with sailors, anglers and picnickers.

Most holidaymakers explore Exmoor from the coastal resorts of Minehead, Ilfracombe, Lynton and Lynmouth. If, however, you want to see the real Exmoor, or what's left of it, you should base your exploration on the Knights' estate village of Simonsbath, the charming town of Dunster, or Dulverton – the modern 'capital' and the headquarters of the National Park authority, originally

Low tide in Lynmouth Harbour

Deepest Somerset – high summer at Luccombe

built as a Poor Law institution. From here, it is easy to set out on foot for Williamson's 'high country of the winds' and to look down on the shimmering waters of the Bristol Channel with the dim blue outline of the South Wales coast on the horizon. There are over 600 miles (965km) of public footpaths and bridleways in the National Park, and the Park authority publishes an excellent series of waymarked walking guides and runs an extensive programme of guided walks.

You can reach the highest point of Dunkery Beacon (1,705ft/519m) quite easily as it is only half a mile (0.8km) across the moor from Dunkery Gate on the minor road between Wheddon

Cross and Luccombe. A longer and more pleasant walk can be taken by parking at Webber's Post, a mile south of Luccombe on the same road, then descending to East Water and crossing to ascend Cloutsham Ball. From Cloutsham, continue to Stoke Perc and go across Stoke Ridge to Dicky's Path, which returns with fine views across the Bristol Channel to Webber's Post along the northern edge of Dunkery.

Perhaps the finest walk in the whole of the National Park is that 30 mile (48km) stretch of the northern coastline which now forms part of the 600 mile (965km) South West Coast Path National Trail. It is here that the geology of Exmoor is revealed at a

glance, as the horizontal strata of the mainly Devonian rocks which form the backbone of the area are abruptly terminated by the crashing rollers of the sea. The rocks are mainly slates, grits and sandstones which were laid down as mud and sand up to 400 million years ago in the bed of a primeval ocean. Later earth movements threw them up into the position we see them in today.

The cliffs of the Exmoor coast rise up 1,200ft (366m) straight from the sea, making it the highest coastline in England. The sheltered north-facing cliffs, highest between The Foreland and Porlock Weir, still shelter extensive coastal woodlands which reach right down to the beach in the cleaves and coombes. This means that the birdwatcher can enjoy an unusual mixture of both woodland and sea birds, with woodpeckers and jays rubbing wings with fulmars, oystercatchers and even guillemots and razorbills at the western end of the coast. Here is the most dramatic part of the coastline, between the strange, rugged, dry Valley of the Rocks west of Lynton (thought to have originally been the course of the River Lyn) and Heddon's Mouth, where the River Heddon carves an impressively deep ravine down to the sea. The heavily wooded and thus appropriately named Woody Bay near Martinhoe is one of the scenic highspots of the coastal path, watched over by the

Watersmeet, where the fast-flowing waters of the East Lyn meet Farley Water and Hoaroak Water in a wooded cleave south of Lynton

No longer thought to be prehistoric, the clapper bridge of Tarr Steps over the River Barle is still a popular attraction

beetling cliffs of Wringapeak and Crock Point, while on Holdstone Down and the Great Hangman above Combe Martin Bay the heathland meets the sea, and the smell of the heather mingles with the salt sea tang.

Although Exmoor's land generally 'lies softly', it should never be underestimated – as illustrated by the disastrous floods in 1952 in Lynton and Lynmouth. Thirty people lost their lives after 9in (23cm) of rain fell on the heights of The Chains in 24 hours, turning the normally gentle River Lyn into a furious raging torrent. The results of that flood can still be seen today in the canalised river at Lynmouth and the huge delta which spreads out into the bay.

With an estimated three million day visitors a year, Exmoor is one of the least visited of our National Parks. This is hard to understand because its charms are endless and the variety of its scenery often spectacularly surprising. Too many of those who do come throng the summertime honeypots of Blackmore's 'Lorna Doone Country' in the Badgworthy valley south of Malmsmead and Oare – the scene of the tragically interrupted wedding of Lorna and John Ridd – or they clog the narrow approach road to the famous clapper bridge of Tarr Steps which crosses the River Barle west of Dulverton. For lovers of Exmoor's solitude, these are places to be avoided in the height of summer.

Blackmore himself wrote of his masterpiece: 'If I had dreamed that it would ever be more than a book of the moment, the descriptions of scenery – which I know as well as I know my garden – would have been kept nearer to their fact. I romanced herein, not to mislead any other, but solely for the uses of story.' That has not stopped generations of tourists following the Lorna Doone Trail, and it is a fact that many of the nefarious activities attributed to Carver Doone were based on the atrocities of a bandit family of the same name who lived in the remote valley in the mid-17th century.

Traditions have a habit of lingering long in the goyals and cleaves of Exmoor. When the English folk-song collector Cecil Sharp came to Porlock in the early years of this century he found the locals singing about a girl who had been captured and carried off by Danish sea-raiders. The incident of which they sang occurred in the year AD988.

Porlock Weir overlooks Porlock Bay, west of the village of Porlock itself

Best seen from the river, the 17th-century manor house and its barn make an attractive grouping with the partly Norman, cob-and-flint church

TOLPUDDLE
Dorset

7 MILES (11 KM) NORTH-EAST OF DORCHESTER

The injustices of village society in days gone by can easily be forgotten, so taken are we with the charm and, so often, the apparent prosperity of Britain's villages today. The story of the Tolpuddle Martyrs, however, permeates every corner of this village, making it the best known of several along the valley of the River Piddle or, as Victorian prudes preferred, Puddle.

In 1833, the year in which slavery was abolished in the British colonies, Dorset farmworkers were being given a weekly wage of seven shillings, three shillings less than the minimum agricultural wage in the south of England. The squirearchy was omnipotent. When George Loveless, a Tolpuddle farm labourer and Methodist lay-preacher, attempted to get a higher wage for his fellow workers he was blocked by local squire and Justice of the Peace, James Frampton. The efforts of the Reverend Warren also came to nothing, so Loveless appealed to the trade union movement. The Grand Lodge of

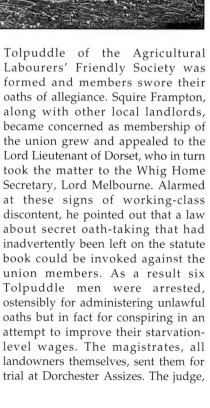

Tolpuddle of the Agricultural Labourers' Friendly Society was formed and members swore their oaths of allegiance. Squire Frampton, along with other local landlords, became concerned as membership of the union grew and appealed to the Lord Lieutenant of Dorset, who in turn took the matter to the Whig Home Secretary, Lord Melbourne. Alarmed at these signs of working-class discontent, he pointed out that a law about secret oath-taking that had inadvertently been left on the statute book could be invoked against the union members. As a result six Tolpuddle men were arrested, ostensibly for administering unlawful oaths but in fact for conspiring in an attempt to improve their starvation-level wages. The magistrates, all landowners themselves, sent them for trial at Dorchester Assizes. The judge,

a Whig and friend of Lord Melbourne, sentenced the men to seven years' transportation to Australia.

George Loveless and his brother James, James Brine, Thomas Stanfield and his son John, and James Hammett, immediately became popular heroes and a nationwide campaign was launched to secure their release. In 1836 the men were granted the king's pardon and returned to this country. Five of them, however, then emigrated to Canada and only James Hammett came back to Tolpuddle, dying a blind man in the workhouse.

Near the centre of the village, on the sloping triangular green, stands an aged sycamore tree under which the martyrs held some of their meetings. Near by, a thatched shelter commemorates the men, as does the gateway to the Methodist chapel. Thomas Standfield's cottage, where their oaths were taken, may be found in the main street, while the whole story is documented in the museum housed in one of the six cottages built beside the main road in 1933 by the Trades Union Council.

Judge Williams Verdict:
'I am not sentencing you for any crime you have committed or that it could be proved that you were about to commit, but as an example to the working-classes of this country.'

The martyrs' tree, an aged sycamore propped up on posts

CORFE CASTLE
Dorset

CORFE CASTLE, 6 MILES (10 KM) SOUTH-EAST OF WAREHAM

Once regarded as one of the finest castles in England, Corfe was reduced during the Civil War to the collection of ragged walls and shattered towers that loom over the small town like broken teeth. After Cromwell's troops had captured this mighty fortress, it was subjected to an unusually brutal 'slighting' that involved undermining anything which could not be blown up with gunpowder. Perhaps this ferocity resulted from the fact that during the first siege of Corfe, the attackers were soundly repelled by Royalist troops under the command of one Lady Bankes. She undertook the defence of the castle in 1643 during her husband's absence, and not only withstood the 500 Parliamentarians and their vast array of weapons and siege equipment, but forced them to retreat leaving 100 of their comrades dead.

The second siege occurred in 1646, conveniently timed when the formidable Lady Bankes was away, but the spirited defenders held out again until eventually the siege was

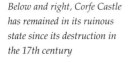

Below and right, Corfe Castle has remained in its ruinous state since its destruction in the 17th century

broken by an act of treachery, rather than military prowess. A small group of soldiers purporting to be Royalists were welcomed into the castle as much-needed additional manpower, but the soldiers were, in fact, Cromwell's men and they hastened to open the gates and allow the besiegers in. As soon as Cromwell's forces had taken the last prisoner, orders were given to destroy the castle so that it would never again withstand a siege.

Building first commenced on Corfe in the 1080s, on a natural hill commanding fine views of the surrounding countryside, and several kings contributed to its stone construction. Most notably, King John paid £1400 for walls, a deep ditch-and-bank defence and his 'gloriette'. Corfe was John's favourite castle and the gloriette was an unfortified residential block containing lavish accommodation for the king, a chapel and offices. Henry III and Edward I added more towers and walls, making Corfe one of the strongest and most powerful castles in the country.

Corfe Castle was particularly important to King John – he imprisoned his wife here and, four years later, he used it as a hiding place for his treasure and crown. He also used it as a prison, and 22 French knights were starved to death within its walls. Other notable prisoners kept at Corfe included Robert of Normandy, William the Conqueror's eldest son, who was kept captive for most of his life by his youngest brother, Henry I. Edward II was also imprisoned here before his fateful journey to Berkeley.

Open daily throughout the year, except Christmas and Boxing Day Tel: 01929 481294.

CHARMOUTH
Dorset

2 MILES (3 KM) EAST OF LYME REGIS

Charmouth Idyll

'...Charmouth, with its high grounds and extensive sweeps of country, and still more its sweet retired bay, backed by dark cliffs, where fragments of low rock among the sands make it the happiest spot for watching the flow of the tide, for sitting in unwearied contemplation.'

Jane Austen, *Persuasion* (1818)

Thatch Lodge is one of the buildings in Charmouth's conservation area

The first complete skeleton of an *ichthyosaurus*, a prehistoric reptile 2lft (7m) long, was discovered in 1811 in the Black Ven cliffs at Charmouth. This part of the coast became a paradise for fossil-hunters, but the cliffs are dangerous to climb. Now summer holidaymakers pack the beach and the grassy meadows where the little River Char makes its way to the sea. To the east the beach runs on to the towering height of Golden Cap. A flat-topped hill of bright orange sandstone, Golden Cap is a distinctive and well-named landmark, and the highest point of land along this coast, at 619 feet (189m). The hill and its surrounding area are cared for by the National Trust. The village of Charmouth is a little way inland, with a long main street that was once a Roman road. One of Charmouth's oldest buildings is the Queen's Arms, used in the Middle Ages by Cistercian monks from Forde Abbey, to which the village belonged. It is named after Catherine of Aragon, Henry VIII's first wife, who apparently stayed here on her arrival in England in 1501. Charles II stayed here, too, as a fugitive some 150 years later.

The tall man's postbox is well out of the sea's reach at Lulworth Cove.

LULWORTH COVE
Dorset

5 MILES (8 KM) SOUTH OF WOOL

Crowded and commercialised as it is in summer, Lulworth Cove remains beautiful. A beauty spot and geology lesson in one, the almost landlocked pool is a natural harbour, formed by the sea biting a narrow gap through the limestone cliff and then scooping out the softer rocks behind. The same process is happening next door to the west, at Stair Hole, and the cliffs all along this stretch of coast are unstable. Durdle Door is a great rock arch carved out over aeons of time by the sea, which can be seen from the coastal path above, or from one of the boats that bring visitors here in the summer. Not surprisingly, perhaps, this lonely shore was once a prime place for smuggling, and the Heritage Centre at Lulworth Cove has displays about this and other aspects of the past. The villages of West and East Lulworth and an extensive army camp lie inland. To the east is the live firing range of the Royal Armoured Corps, where much of the early development work on tanks was carried out. On non-firing days the road and marked footpaths across the range are open, and there is access to the forlorn, deserted village of Tyneham, which was evacuated during World War II when the range was extended.

ILSINGTON HOUSE
Dorset

PUDDLETOWN, 4½ MILES (7 KM) NORTH-EAST OF DORCHESTER

Below right, the rather severe grey-harled exterior of Ilsington belies its bright interior; above, the elegant dining room

*I*ts royal scandal aside, Ilsington House is more fascinating than its grey, symmetrical façade might suggest, and this is largely due to the splendid restoration work of recent years and the interesting art collection which now adorns its walls. The house is almost pure William and Mary, apart from some 18th-century plasterwork and fireplaces and Victorian additions, and is furnished with fine period pieces.

It was its architectural purity which attracted Peter and Penelope Duff to the house, which they bought in 1979 after an eight-year search for their ideal property. When they moved in a year later, however, they were still without carpets, curtains and furniture as the house had been empty for two years and was in need of restoration, which is an ongoing process. Once in residence, Penelope Duff set about displaying the splendid paintings and sculptures which she had been amassing since the age of 12. It is a fascinating and extensive collection containing both classic and modern works, including signed lithographs by Toulouse Lautrec and a painting of Lew Hoad by Cecil Beaton. There are also a number of works by Peter Mahone, of the Ruralist group, work by Panayiotis Kalorkoti, the official war artist for the Falklands War, and recent works by students of the Royal Academy School. Sculptures include work by Elisabeth Frink and Serena de la Hey.

The scandal involved Princess Sophia, a daughter of George III. Between 1792 and 1830 Ilsington was leased to General Thomas Garth, the King's Principal Equerry who, like many other courtiers, took houses in the area in order to be near the monarch during his summer sojourns in Weymouth. Sophia and two of her sisters would usually spend the last night of their journeys to Weymouth here. In 1800 Princess Sophia gave birth, in Weymouth, to a son who was promptly adopted by a local couple. General Garth adopted the boy when

he was two years old and brought him up at Ilsington. Young Thomas received some financial support from his mother, though his attempt to formalise the arrangement came to nothing and in the process he was tricked out of his possession of documents which proved his noble birth. In pursuing his claim further, the scandal broke in the press and the royal family eventually settled £3,000 a year for life on the boy. Though Tom's paternity was never revealed, suspicion fell naturally on General Garth – despite the fact that he was 30 years older than Sophia and far from attractive.

Open from May to September on selected afternoons. Tel: 01305 848454.

The herbaceous bed runs along the edge of the Long Pond

FORDE ABBEY
Dorset

4 MILES (6.5 KM) EAST OF CHARD

Close to the banks of the Axe, which marks the county boundary between Somerset and Dorset, are the splendid gardens of Forde Abbey. Occupied as a private house since 1649, the former Cistercian abbey buildings are set in a beautiful and varied garden. Bright borders are backed by honey-coloured stone walls, and wide sloping lawns are punctuated by mature trees, while a chain of ponds, once the monks' fish ponds, now feature cascades and are embellished with statuary.

Entering through the walled gardens where the excellent nursery is housed, around the side of the abbey, the first view leads up to a statue flanked by two yews at the end of two deep, immensely colourful flower borders. With the Long Pond running along the back of the left-hand herbaceous bed, the eye is drawn to the enormous variation of height and colour provided by the statuesque *Nicotiana sylvestris* jostling with shrub roses, hydrangeas and irises, underplanted with salvias, silver stachys, tradescants and many others. Beyond is the Mount, from the top of which you can enjoy a wonderful birds'-eye view back over the Long Pond and the cone-shaped, clipped yews on either side of the herbaceous borders. The Mount itself is dominated by trees, including a great redwood *Sequoia sempervirens* and the incense cedar, *Calocedrus decurrens.*

The path runs through parkland further to the north and, after tantalising views of the 4 acre (1.6ha) Great Pond, enters the bog garden created from an area of the pond that has been silted up for centuries. In this, one of the most beautiful areas of the gardens, you can see a wide range of variegated grasses, astilbes, the ruby-coloured lobelia, meconopsis, irises and, dotted around, masses of elegant candelabra primulas overhung by giant gunnera and rustling bamboo.

At the southern margin of the Great Pond is the remarkable Beech House. It is carved from growing tree trunks, and even has a window overlooking the lake. On the return journey towards the abbey buildings you pass an 18th-century ha-ha, a ditch dug to keep animals within the park without the view being interrupted by a fence. The rock garden was created out of an old gravel pit before World War I, and supports many interesting plants, including a *Hydrangea petiolaris* which climbs a thorn tree beside the top pool.

In an area that boasts many fine gardens, those at Forde Abbey stand out as being not only beautiful, but also notable for the many rare plants which have been laid out to complement the attractive stone of the abbey buildings.

Open all year. Tel: 01460 221366.

Part of the water garden (below), and the magnificent rock garden

BROADLANDS
Dorset

4 MILES (6.5 KM) SOUTH OF STURMINSTER NEWTON

Three different views of Broadlands, showing the rich variety of planting and structure in this attractive garden

Set in the rolling countryside of central Dorset, the gardens of Broadlands, at Hazelbury Bryan, skilfully conceal the fact that their full extent is only 2 acres (0.8ha). The design and planting of the garden has occupied the owners, Mr and Mrs M J Smith, for the past 17 years. Although no tricks of layout seem to be involved apart from the use of screening hedges, there are sudden views of the ornamental woodland and the vegetable garden, and the main lawn is broken up by island beds, creating a network of bays or small 'garden rooms' with an informal structure.

Much of the area in front of the vine-covered house is given over to lawn with three specimen trees – a variegated holly, a robinia with golden leaves and a Himalayan birch with a dramatic white trunk – while along the roadside hedges a shrub bed provides colour throughout the year. On the north side of the house grassy glades lead into a woodland area where fast-growing native and ornamental trees have been established and then underplanted with azaleas, rhododendrons, camellias and hydrangeas – all of which have now been underplanted in their turn by daffodils, hellebores and hostas.

The woodland is separated from a large lawn by a great beech hedge 120ft (36.5m) long and 8ft (2.4m) high.

Among the enclosed areas that break up the lawn is a cottage garden strikingly planted with geraniums, salvias, rock roses and echinops, together with other flowers chosen to give colour throughout the year. A recent development has been the creation of a large conservation pond and associated water garden, which adds greatly to the attractions of Broadlands. Now, colonies of frogs, toads, newts and dragonflies have settled the area, and wading birds also visit on occasions.

An archway gives access to a new rose garden featuring trellis and a curving pergola draped with climbing roses chosen for their fragrance as well as their colour, and with clematis contributing to the overall colour scheme of pink, white, crimson and silver. Shrub roses are naturalised in grass so that their fragrance can be appreciated at close quarters.

Broadlands is not only a charming country garden with appeal to the visitor at every season, it also has many unusual plants to intrigue the plant lover. It might even be described as an arboretum, as there are fine magnolias, viburnums, dogwoods and hollies, and, more important still, the plants are carefully labelled.

Open from June to August on selected days. Tel: 01258 817374.

WORTH MATRAVERS
Dorset

3 MILES (5 KM) WEST OF SWANAGE

In the churchyard is the grave of one Benjamin Jesty, who is said to have used his wife and sons as guinea-pigs, inoculating them with cowpox against smallpox. This was in 1774, some 24 years before Sir Edward Jenner published the findings of his similar experiments.

Sunshine lifts the otherwise somewhat austere stone of the houses

The Isle of Purbeck is pitted with old quarries, quarries that produced Purbeck marble, a limestone that polishes like marble and was used in many medieval churches and cathedrals. All the houses of Worth Matravers, built of this greyish stone, were once the homes of local quarrymen and stonemasons. A little uphill from the duck pond is The Square and Compass Inn, which takes its name from the tools of the stonemason's craft, and many of the garden walls display an ammonite or two, revealed during quarrying. Dry-stone walls criss-cross the somewhat treeless landscape that surrounds the compact little village. A short walk down the narrow valley at the head of which it stands (with good views of extensive strip lynchets on either side) leads to clifftop Winspit Quarry, now disused. Stone from here was lowered directly on to sea barges and taken round to Swanage for transport on to London. Swanage was originally just a hamlet in the parish of Worth Matravers, the two churches being connected by a path, now known as The Priest's Way. Worth Matravers Church is especially fine. It needed restoration work in the 19th century, but its tympanum, depicting the Coronation of the Virgin, its beautiful, ornate chancel arch and some windows all date from Norman times.

Roses round the door of one of the thatched cottages

BURTON BRADSTOCK
Dorset

3 MILES (5 KM) SOUTH-EAST OF BRIDPORT

The Dorset historian Hutchins made the perhaps doubtful claim that in 1757 a mermaid was washed up on the beach here. However, the charm of the village that lies just inland from the western end of Chesil Beach is something that remains beyond question. Narrow lanes wiggle and wind away from the main road, all packed with pretty houses, their roofs neatly thatched or tiled in local Purbeck stone-slate. The walls of rubble limestone, some colour-washed, are often clad in roses, clematis or ivy. Many of the houses are 17th-century, including the White House by the triangular green, while the Perpendicular church with its central tower dates entirely to the 15th century, except for the surprising and idiosyncratic south aisle designed by E S Prior at the end of the 19th century. The little River Bride works its way through the village to pass though a gap in the cliffs about a mile south. The hills behind the village, some of which have prehistoric hillforts on top, all offer good views over the English Channel. Mermaids or no, smuggling was rife along this stretch of coast in the 18th century and the county's most notorious smuggler, Isaac Gulliver, used the Drove Inn as his contraband distribution centre.

Cottages line the Nunney Brook

NUNNEY
Somerset

3 MILES (4.8 KM) SOUTH-WEST OF FROME

The Village of Nunney
... perfection, having everything which the heart could desire to make it both lovely and interesting...
Maxwell Fraser

*I*t is not often a village can add a moated medieval castle to a list of ingredients that already satisfies every requirement of a fairy-tale village. But Nunney is exceptional. It is set in a wooded valley at the eastern end of the Mendip Hills; a stream flows past the grey-stone, red-tiled houses and thatched cottages; there is a church on the hill, a fine manor house and a pub. It even has a thatched bus shelter.

The castle dates to 1373, when Sir John De la Mare, recently returned from the war in France with much booty, was given a licence to fortify and crenellate his manse. He placed four mighty, round towers at the corners of a rectangular central block four storeys high. Pevsner says it is of a type found in the north of England; others say it was modelled on the Bastille in France. During the Civil Wars it was a Royalist stronghold and was eventually beaten into submission by Parliamentarian cannon. Today the romantic ruin, in the care of English Heritage, is reached from the main street by a foot-bridge over what is said to be the deepest water-filled moat in the country. Across the stream and the street from the castle is the church, originally 13th-century but much rebuilt in the 19th century. It has a round Norman font, bits of a Saxon cross and a wall-painting of St George. There are effigies of Sir John (probably) and of subsequent owners of the castle, the Poulets and the Praters. One of the Roundhead cannonballs that wrecked the castle is on display. The Nunney Brook flows down the length of the village and it was this that first brought the village prosperity, when the wool trade was centred on nearby Frome in the late 17th and early 18th centuries. Many of the weavers' cottages in Horn Street carry dates within this period and most of the bigger houses were also built at this time, including Palladian-style Manor Farm. Wool was washed on the sloping cobbled pavement in front of the church, where the medieval market cross stands. The industry declined locally towards the end of the 18th century when mills in the North took all the trade, but at about that time Fussell's ironworks grew up, using the Nunney Brook for power and providing employment well into the 19th century.

The ruined castle and its moat

New housing in a sympathetic style

LUCCOMBE
Somerset

4 MILES (6.5 KM) SOUTH-EAST OF PORLOCK

During the Civil War, Parliamentarians tried to arrest Luccombe's Royalist vicar, Henry Byam. He escaped, however, to join Charles I. At the Restoration, Byam was returned as Vicar of Luccombe, Canon of Exeter and Prebendary of Wales, to much local rejoicing.

*L*uccombe is one of the prettiest villages on the Holnicote Estate, an area of Exmoor beneath Dunkery Beacon that is owned by the National Trust. Steep, narrow lanes lead to the village through fields of red earth bounded by red sandstone walls. It is the cottages that make Luccombe attractive. Most are of cob, cream-washed with a black skirting at the base, and have uneven thatched roofs with overhanging eaves.Until it was given to the National Trust in 1944, the Holnicote Estate was owned by the Acland family. In the early 19th century the 10th Baronet Acland did much to improve the estate and many of the 16th- and 17th-century cottages were extended by raising the roofs, making attic rooms with dormer windows. Rounded bread ovens, projecting from one corner, can still be seen on some cottages. In recent years a few new houses have been built in sympathetic style by a local housing association, to provide accommodation in an area where few local people can afford it any more. The church is a good one – high and light, with a wagon roof decorated with large bosses and some glass in Arts and Crafts style. It is depicted in Samuel Palmer's famous painting, 'Coming out of Evening Church'.

MONTACUTE HOUSE
Somerset

MONTACUTE, 4 MILES (6.5 KM) WEST OF YEOVIL

*Montacute House, a
beautiful home rescued from
the scrap heap*

Montacute House is one of Britain's best-preserved Elizabethan mansions – an impressive edifice of glittering glass interspersed with the golden glow of Ham Hill stone. It was built around the end of the 16th century for Sir Edward Phelips, a lawyer who rose to be Speaker of the House of Commons and Master of the Rolls (it was he who opened for the Prosecution at the trial of Guy Fawkes).

The interior of the house is no less impressive than its beautiful, symmetrical exterior. There are decorated ceilings, splendidly ornate fireplaces, heraldic glass and fine wood panelling, but by the time the property came to the National Trust the original contents had, sadly, been dispersed. In fact, the house itself was nearly lost – in 1931, after years of neglect, it was on the market for £5,882 'for scrap'! Rescue came in the form of a Mr E Cook who donated sufficient funds to the Society for the Protection of Ancient Buildings to buy Montacute and to present it to the National Trust.

Today, the rooms are suitably furnished thanks to various loans and bequests, and the Long Gallery – at 172ft (52.2m) the largest surviving gallery in the country – houses a magnificent collection of Elizabethan and Jacobean paintings on permanent loan from the National Portrait Gallery.

Open from Easter to October daily, except Tuesday. Tel: 01935 823289.

HESTERCOMBE HOUSE GARDENS
Somerset

CHEDDON FITZPAINE, 2 MILES (3 KM) NORTH-EAST OF TAUNTON

Lutyens' elegant orangery gives a focus to the garden

Set high on a south-facing slope overlooking the valley of the River Tone, with distant views of the Blackdown Hills in Somerset, are the gardens of Hestercombe House. They are one of the best surviving examples of the collaboration between Sir Edwin Lutyens and Gertrude Jekyll, built for the Hon E W B Portman between 1903 and 1908, and now owned and maintained with sensitivity by Somerset County Council as the headquarters for the county fire service.

The gaunt house and upper terrace were already in existence when Lutyens came to Hestercombe, and the dynamic of his design was to concentrate the garden interest to the south, fully engaging the magnificent views over the surrounding country-

side. By the use of a classical open-air rotunda, he changed the direction of the 19th-century terrace to include a baroque orangery of great elegance, which he himself designed, and a Dutch garden. Lutyens used local materials, such as Morte slate from behind the house, and golden limestone from Ham Hill near Yeovil, and introduced flights of circular steps to create spaciousness. Water, too, was used to create tranquillity, and rills run from recessed ponds – to the west through a rose garden, and to the east from the rotunda pool.

From quite early on in her career Miss Jekyll was extremely myopic, and her planting at Hestercombe and elsewhere was concerned with the texture, overall shape and perfume of plants, as well as with their colour. The

Grey Walk, below the upper terrace, is planted throughout in soft colours. Greys, silver, mauve and white predominate, with lavender, rosemary and pinks interplanted with catmint, while strongly scented choisyas are used at the end of the border, and yuccas and blue thistles give structure to the overall composition.

The central area has a formal layout with beds filled with pink roses that contrast sharply with the strong leaves of the surrounding *Bergenia cordifolia*.

Peonies, lilies and delphiniums catch the eye, and a pergola overhung with climbing roses, honeysuckle and clematis creates a fragrant as well as a colourful and shady path in summer. Characteristic of Lutyens's attention to detail are the circular windows cut in the south walls of the pergola, and the alternately square and circular pillars that hold up the cross-beams of the structure.

Open all year, except Christmas and New Year. Tel: 0823 337222.

Below left, roses and clematis intertwine above the pathway

Below, detail of a bearded waterspout

HADSPEN HOUSE
Somerset

2 MILES (3 KM) SOUTH-EAST OF CASTLE CARY

Set in the lush Somerset countryside, Hadspen is a fine garden with a distinguished pedigree. The manor house was built of the golden Ham stone of the area by the Hobhouse family in the 18th century, but the basic structure of the garden was established by Margaret Hobhouse in the great days of British gardening at the end of the last century. After some decades of neglect, the well-known gardening writer and designer, Penelope Hobhouse, undertook restoration. The property is now owned by Mr Niall Hobhouse, and the garden and nursery are managed by Mr and Mrs Pope.

As the main garden is now separated from the house, which is not open to the public, the visitor enters at the highest point of a south-facing slope, where there is a splendid lily pond created by Penelope Hobhouse out of a large water tank. Here, in raised beds set in gravel, silver plants such as stachys, thyme and purple sage predominate. The old walled kitchen garden has been filled by Mr and Mrs Pope with shrubs and herbaceous plants rather than with vegetables, and a border with tall shrubs and climbers runs along a wall leading down into the valley. Hadspen holds the national collection of rodgersias, and in this shady dell you can see some of the best varieties, including *R. pinnata* 'Superba' and *R. sambucifolia*. Near by, a double border is protected by beech hedges which were planted specifically to create good conditions for the extensive collection of hostas, including the cultivars 'Hadspen Blue' and 'Hadspen Heron'.

Beyond a bisecting gravel path edged with catmint, the borders are planted with yellow-flowering herbaceous plants – yellow lupins, roses and hypericum, Jerusalem sage and rock roses. Just as striking, with its silver- and grey-leaved plants, is the border which faces the kitchen garden. Senecios, santolinas and artemisias contrast with a morning glory bush and with eleagnus.

You can follow the bamboo path past the Victorian summerhouse to a small pond, then continue up alongside Victorian shrubberies, past a meadow area which supports fritillaries in spring and orchids in early summer, to a late 19th-century fountain where an earlier Hobhouse laid out a terrace in the Italian style with ornate stone-work and beds for annuals. As would be expected at a garden of the quality of Hadspen, changes are continually being made, and many plants not otherwise readily found can be purchased in the nursery.

Open from March to October on selected days. Tel: 01963 50939.

Left and top, the gardens at Hadspen show a wide variety of planting, including the sprawling catmint borders (above), backed with white roses

WEST SOMERSET RAILWAY
Somerset

BISHOPS LYDEARD, 5 MILES (8 KM) NORTH-WEST OF TAUNTON

Stretching for 20 miles (32km) between Bishops Lydeard and Minehead, the West Somerset Railway is the longest preserved railway in Britain. It may one day be even longer, for there is still a connection with the main line to the west of Taunton station for the occasional through excursion. For the time being, however, passengers arriving by train at Taunton are usually met by a connecting bus which takes them to the eastern terminus at Bishops Lydeard.

The existence of this railway is due to the initiative of the county council,

Bishops Lydeard station

which purchased the line following its closure by British Rail in 1971. This enabled the West Somerset Railway to refurbish the route and re-open it in stages between 1976 and 1979. It retains the atmosphere of a Great Western Railway single-track holiday branch – indeed it became so busy during the summer months that two special passing loops had to be built to break up sections between stations, and the platform at Minehead was lengthened to accommodate 16-coach trains. This legacy has stood the railway in good stead, for it needs to run long trains during the peak holiday season to cope with the volume of travellers. Passengers at Bishops Lydeard have plenty to occupy their time, for there is a visitor centre in the former goods shed, incorporating a locomotive or coach, a working signalbox and signals, photographs, railway memorabilia and a model railway.

Northbound trains have a stiff climb for 4 miles (6.5km) to the highest point of the line at Crowcombe Heathfield, where the station has two platforms and a separate stationmaster's house with decorative bargeboards. Views of the Quantock and Brendon Hills open up to the left before arrival at Stogumber, seemingly a good example of minimalist station design, with its tiny platform shelter – in fact the station building is unusually positioned at ground level on the opposite side of the track to the platform. At this station passengers can take advantage of a picnic site in lovely surroundings. The half-way station of Williton has two architectural delights for connoisseurs of industrial buildings – it has the only surviving operational Bristol & Exeter Railway signal box, and a very early metal-framed prefabricated structure which was dismantled at Swindon

The smart cream and chocolate-brown paintwork of the railway's coaches

The line near Crowcombe, which has one of the railway's ten stations

railway works and re-erected here. A listed building, it now provides covered accommodation for rolling stock.

Beyond Williton the train comes within 15yds (13m) of the sea at high tide, and as it approaches Watchet station it skirts the harbour on the right. Still active with commercial shipping up to 2500 tons, Watchet is the oldest port in the county and has recently celebrated its millenium. It was the prime reason for the railway, which arrived here in 1862, and the extension to Minehead took another 12 years to complete. It was in the docks at Watchet that Coleridge is believed to have found inspiration for *The Rime of the Ancient Mariner* in his conversations with sailors. Energetic passengers equipped for walking can leave the train here, or at the next station, Washford, to explore the remains of the West Somerset Mineral Railway. This fascinating line was built primarily to convey iron ore extracted from the Brendon Hills to Watchet harbour for shipment across the Bristol Channel to the foundries of south Wales. The most interesting

part is the section from Comberow, where an inclined plane ascended the slope of the hills.

Leaving Watchet the line turns inland and crosses the trackbed of the mineral railway before reaching Washford, where there is a small museum commemorating the Somerset & Dorset Railway, a route which once ran through the Mendips from Bath to Bournemouth. The line returns to the sea as it nears Blue Anchor, where the waiting room houses a museum of GWR artefacts. With marvellous views out to sea, the line hugs the shore to Dunster. A break in the 1-hour 20-minute journey to walk up the road to this attractive and interesting village is strongly recommended.

A long straight takes the railway past the largest holiday centre in the country and into the terminus and headquarters of the railway, where locomotives and carriages are repaired. Old Minehead and the 17th-century harbour are both the stuff of picture postcards.

Train service: most days between Easter and October, daily from June–September. Tel: 01643 707650.

The signal box at Washford

The pleasing frontage of Dyrham Park, now in the care of the National Trust

DYRHAM PARK
Avon

DYRHAM, 8 MILES (13 KM) NORTH OF BATH

T here was once a Tudor house on this site, but the Dyrham Park we see today, built for William Blathwayt, is entirely a creation of the William and Mary period. Blathwayt rose from fairly modest beginnings through the Civil Service to hold a number of top government jobs and found favour with William III both for his administrative abilities and because he spoke Dutch. Blathwayt also made an advantageous marriage to the heiress of the Dyrham estate, but it was not until after the death of both his in-laws and his wife that he began to replace their family home.

The mansion was constructed in two stages, first in 1692 by an unknown Huguenot architect, and around the turn of the century by one of the foremost architects of the day, William Talman. Between them they created a splendid house which displays unusual restraint for the times.

Dyrham Park has changed little over the years and all the furniture, paintings and pottery we see in the house today were collected by Blathwayt himself. The series of apartments are decorated and furnished very much with a Dutch influence, including paintings of the Dutch school and a collection of blue-and-white Delft ware. There are Dutch-style gardens, too.

Open from April to October daily, except Wednesday and Thursday. Tel: 0117 9372501.

CHEW MAGNA
Avon

6 MILES (9.5 KM) SOUTH OF BRISTOL

'I t is a praty clothing town, and hath a faire church,' wrote John Leland, reporting on Chew Magna to Henry VIII in 1545. It is still a pretty village today, but any air of prosperity probably has more to do with proximity to Bristol than the cloth trade. The church, partly Norman, is, as so often, the strongest link with the wool era. It is memorable chiefly for the 15th-century tower and its fiercesome gang of gargoyles. Inside is a large rood screen, and a wooden tomb effigy over which an air of mystery hangs. It claims to be Sir John de Hauteville, and he lies, rather uncomfortably, on his side, propped up on one elbow, legs crossed, one foot resting on an upright lion. He wears 14th-century armour, but other details do not tie up with that date. Near the church is a striking 16th-century building known either as the Old Schoolroom (for that is what it was from 1842 to 1894) or the Church Alehouse, one-time venue for parish parties. Chew Court, once part of the Bishop of Bath and Wells's Palace of Chew, has an imposing gateway above which is the old courtroom. The High Street is flanked by unusual raised pavements, some good Georgian houses and pleasant cottages.

Tun Bridge
A buttress on the eastern side of the bridge holds a stone trough 'well'. When smallpox was rife in the village this was filled with disinfectant and farmers, bringing their goods for sale only as far as the bridge, would collect their money from the well.

The shaft of an old preaching cross in the churchyard

VINE HOUSE
Avon

HENBURY, 4 MILES (6.5 KM) NORTH-WEST OF BRISTOL

The orchard may be glimpsed through the greenery, with the church tower beyond

Close to the centre of Bristol, Vine House has the good fortune to be on the edge of the Blaise Castle estate – which was landscaped by Humphry Repton – alongside the Hazel Brook, a tributary of the River Trym. Even allowing for the well-wooded acres of the 18th-century park, the immediate urban surroundings of The Vine are somewhat unprepossessing, but once behind the creeper-clad stone house it is easy to see what appealed to Professor T F Hewer and his wife, Anne, when they first began to design the layout in 1946.

The 2 acre (0.8ha) garden is divided roughly into two parts: the upper lawn is given a wonderful sense of enclosure and shape by the two magnolias – one against the house and the other near the stables – by the great mulberry, and by tall conifers standing at the back of the herbaceous border. Further down a stream, bright with colourful bog plants such as *Lysichiton americanus* and irises, flows over rocks, past a small arbour and under a stone bridge to the slow-moving brook. In the lower part of the garden the owners have created a peaceful green glade with spring bulbs, cyclamen, and an abundance of hostas, cistus and gunnera.

In two respects Vine House is an important as well as a beautiful garden. When they started work, Professor and Mrs Hewer reduced the site to bare earth and planned the position and eventual size of the trees with the help of sticks topped by pieces of white paper. As the head of the Department of Pathology, Professor Hewer regularly travelled abroad to conferences and brought back with him specimen trees which have now matured. Carefully labelled and dated, the trees at Vine House constitute a remarkable arboretum, including as they do a 30ft (9m)

Metasequoia glyptostroboides and a splendid weeping pine from Yugo-slavia, introduced in 1951 and now underplanted with cyclamen. Together with Chinese specimens, a Japanese cherry, and a noble *Acer capillipes* grown from seed obtained from the Westonbirt Arboretum in 1957, this is an important collection of trees in its own right.

Vine House is a memorable garden at any stage of the year, but particularly so in the spring and early summer. When the bulbs are at their best, the garden boasts an unusually tall snowdrop with bell-shaped, white flowers on a leafless stem. Then, as the days lengthen, a pale smoke bush and hybrid tree peonies take over, filling this peaceful woodland garden with subtle colour.

Open all year daily by appointment only. Tel: 0117 9503573.

Left, a comfortably overgrown path and a profusion of flowers (below) characterise this charming garden

AVEBURY
Wiltshire

6 MILES (9.5 KM WEST) OF MARLBOROUGH

In 1663 the diarist John Aubrey wrote that the prehistoric site of Avebury 'does as much exceed Stonehenge in greatness as a cathedral does a parish church'. The 28 acre (11.3ha) complex is indeed very much larger and arguably more impressive than that of its more famous and now, sadly, somewhat tawdry sister. It also predates Stonehenge, making it the place, according to Sir John Betjeman, where the story of English architecture begins.

Sarsen stones at the door of the Red Lion

To enter this unique village and observe its daily life, apparently unaffected by the immense Neolithic stone circle within which it partly stands, is to feel the centuries concertina into timelessness. The circle, with its gaunt stones and its vast bank and ditch, was probably in use as a major ceremonial centre from c.2500BC. In the early Middle Ages, however, with the arrival of the first Christian chapel at Avebury, villagers set about burying some of the pagan stones. By the 18th century, when the village was expanding, other stones were broken up and these squarish blocks of sarsen can be seen in several of the buildings, including the old school, Silbury House and the Methodist chapel. As recently as the early 1960s the National Trust seriously considered demolishing parts of the village within the circle, including the manorial aisled barn that now houses the Museum of Wiltshire Folk Life. The uneasy partnership between village and prehistoric site seems now to have settled into mutual forbearance, with the thatched pub plying its trade in the shadow of the stones. The church, of Saxon and Norman origins, is remarkable for its south doorway, font and rood screen, and sits prettily with the Elizabethan manor house just outside the earthwork. Other attractive houses within and without the circle are built of brick, flint or cob, some timber-framed, several thatched.

LACOCK ABBEY
Wiltshire

LACOCK, 3 MILES (5 KM) SOUTH OF CHIPPENHAM

When Lacock Abbey was given to the National Trust in 1944 it came with a whole village, and a more delightful and complementary assemblage would be hard to find. The abbey was founded in 1232 and continued as an Augustinian nunnery until Henry VIII dissolved the monasteries in 1539.

Like many other religious foundations, Lacock was converted into a private residence, but unlike most others it has retained a large proportion of its monastic buildings, including the cloisters, chapter house and sacristy. And where many similar properties were changed beyond recognition, Lacock was converted with care and sensitivity, though some of its features are Gothic Revival rather than pure medieval. It is furnished with some interesting pieces, including a chair which is said to have been used in the camp of Charles I, and a pair of 18th-century leather chests. Also on display is a photographic copy of the Lacock Abbey Magna Carta (the original is in the British Museum).

For most of its secular life Lacock Abbey was owned by the Talbot family, whose most famous member was William Henry Fox Talbot, the pioneer of photography who invented the photographic negative here. The middle window in the south gallery was the subject of Fox Talbot's earliest existing negative, and there is a Museum of Photography in the gatehouse.

Open from April to end-October every afternoon, except Tuesday. Tel: 01249 730227.

Fine vaulting adorns the old cloisters

The splendid old Elizabethan house of Longleat has seen many changes, including the development of a safari and wildlife park in the grounds

LONGLEAT
Wiltshire

5 MILES (8 KM) WEST OF WARMINSTER

The man who built Longleat was truly remarkable. In the space of just 40 years John Thynne rose from working in Henry VIII's kitchen to entertaining Queen Elizabeth I at his vast mansion. Single-mindedly ambitious and cleverly persuasive, he acquired both social position and great wealth and laid the foundations of a dynasty which still occupies the vast country estate originally purchased for £53. When the new house, which he designed himself, was destroyed by fire the determined Thynne simply bought a quarry of Bath stone and started again.

Colourful characters have always populated Longleat. John Thynne's son, a lazy and violent man, was fined for fraud and the mismanagement of his public duties; a later heir married a woman who, though of noble birth, was so disreputable that her behaviour shocked even Charles II and she was banned from Court; the next heir was murdered by assassins hired by an admirer of his wife; another eloped with the daughter of a local toll-keeper. And yet, though so many of the guardians of Longleat could easily have led caused its downfall, every so often there came a descendant who was worthy of John Thynne. The 1st Viscount Weymouth was such a man. Of modest habits and a devoted husband, he built up the estate and created wonderful gardens, sadly destroyed in one generation by his successor who neglected both house and grounds. The 3rd Viscount found favour at the Court of George III, who elevated him to the rank of Marquess of Bath and visited Longleat in 1789. Nevertheless he died in debt and his son, a shrewd businessman, was forced to concentrate all his efforts on saving the estate. He also made substantial improvements to the house, employing James Wyatt to carry out the work which took ten years to complete.

In the history of such a family as this it is difficult to pick out a 'Golden Age', but the Victorian era certainly left its mark here. The estate prospered, high society was lavishly entertained and the state rooms were remodelled in baroque style, with no expense spared. The excellent workmanship is still evident today in the superbly intricate gilded ceilings and the extraordinarily sumptuous and richly decorated rooms. But the development of Longleat did not stop there – the present Lord Bath's apartments are decorated with his own murals, hugely colourful works which display a characteristic lack of restraint.

Open all year daily, except Christmas Day. Tel: 01985 844400.

The lower dining room features a remarkable gilded ceiling

STOURTON HOUSE
Wiltshire

STOURTON, 2 MILES (3 KM) NORTH-WEST OF MERE

Borders colourful with golden achillea in the gardens at Stourton

It says much for the charm and beauty of Stourton House gardens that they can stand comparison with the magnificent landscaped grounds of Stourhead only a matter of 300 yards away. In 5 acres (2ha) many plant treasures, accommodated in a series of small, friendly spaces, are to be seen. Stourton is also a garden with a purpose: to produce flowers and foliage for drying, with up to 70 per cent of the plants produced being dried and turned into beautiful bouquets.

There is a historical connection between the two gardens as, in late Georgian times, a parson of Stourton married one of the Miss Hoares of Stourhead and money from the banking family went into constructing Stourton House and laying out a garden. But it was not until Colonel and Mrs Bullivant came to live here 30 years ago, and flower-drying became the business of the house, that the gardens really took on their present character.

Now the main gardens lie on the east side of the house, and visitors are recommended to start their tour in the kitchen garden where the beds contain not only vegetables, but also a range of

Bog plants include the carnivorous pitcher plant, flowering rushes and groups of lovely water iris, both yellow and purple, and around the margins are rock roses, mimulus and carnations. The surrounding beds are overflowing with tree peonies, hydrangeas, standard roses, perennial honesty, and the meadow foam offers colour throughout the season.

To the south of the Pool Garden is the Lower Pond Garden, where daffodils and narcissus dominate in spring, and near by there is a pocket handkerchief tree, *Davidia involucrata*, and a splendid *Magnolia liliiflora* 'Nigra', which boasts purple flowers. Beyond the south lawn and the 19th-century greenhouse, perhaps a relic of the link with the Hoare family, is a woodland garden covered in hostas and different species of hydrangea.

This is a fascinating garden, with meandering paths through the different sections giving constant surprise and interest. Many plants have self-seeded, like the brightly coloured poached-egg plant, to give Stourton a true cottage feel as well as a formal one.

Open from April to November, on selected days. Tel: 01747 840417.

The flame-coloured nasturtium Tropaeolum speciosum grows spectacularly in the hedge

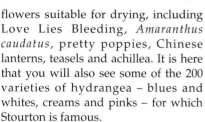

flowers suitable for drying, including Love Lies Bleeding, *Amaranthus caudatus*, pretty poppies, Chinese lanterns, teasels and achillea. It is here that you will also see some of the 200 varieties of hydrangea – blues and whites, creams and pinks – for which Stourton is famous.

On either side of the path leading down to the Lily Pond garden are great Lawson cypresses known as the Twelve Apostles. The central pool is surrounded by beds of shrubs and herbaceous plants, while the flower fountain in the centre consists of a stone dish filled with unusual plants.

BOWOOD
Wiltshire

CALNE, 5 MILES (8 KM) EAST OF CHIPPENHAM

Bowood is one of the West Country's favourite estates – a fine house set in a wonderful 'Capability' Brown landscape which offers a new delight at every turn. It is occupied today by the Earl of Shelburne, son of the 8th Marquess of Lansdowne, and though he is the first of his family to make Bowood his permanent home the house offers a great insight into the lives of his ancestors and their passion for fine art and literature.

Since the time of the 1st Marquess, in the 18th century, the family has been committed to public service, producing a succession of great men who have distinguished themselves in high political office – a Prime Minister, a Chancellor of the Exchequer, a Governor General of Canada and a Viceroy of India. And yet, in addition to their great involvement in affairs of the state, the successive Lords Lansdowne all found the time to be avid collectors of fine paintings and sculpture, and fascinating heirlooms.

The orangery, designed by Robert Adam and once full of orange and lemon trees, now contains part of the Landsowne collection of paintings and a series of busts, while the sculpture gallery houses a variety of exceptional works, including some collected by the 1st Marquess. The two 16th-century Brussels tapestries on the walls are the

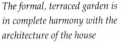

The formal, terraced garden is in complete harmony with the architecture of the house

fairly recent acquisitions of the present Earl of Shelburne. Off the orangery is a small room known as the laboratory, and it was here that Joseph Priestley, tutor to the 1st Lord Lansdowne's two sons, discovered oxygen. John Ingenhouse later discovered the process of photosynthesis in plants here, and carried out pioneering work on smallpox vaccine.

The exhibition galleries upstairs include a fascinating collection of items from the 5th Lord Lansdowne's time in India; the Georgian Exhibition Room is set out as it would have been in the time of the 1st Marquess, complete with figures dressed from the Lansdowne costume collection, while the Victorian Room would have been familiar to the 3rd Marquess. Beyond these is the fabulous collection of family jewels.

Bowood is a splendid house, but it is actually only a part of the building which stood here until as recently as 1955. The house which had developed and expanded with the growing prosperity of its owners over a 200-year period had finally become unmanageable, and in order to save the estate as a whole the 'Big House' was demolished. As a memorial to those great men, however, Bowood is undiminished.

Open from 30 March to 27 October daily. Tel: 01249 812102.

The graceful Orangery serves as a picture gallery

Robert Adam's original drawings for what is now the sculpture gallery show pens for wild animals, and family records detail the sad demise of an orang-utan at Christmas in 1768. Jeremy Bentham, the philosopher, visiting the house in 1781, spoke of going to stroke the leopard!

MOMPESSON HOUSE
Wiltshire

SALISBURY, 21 MILES (34 KM) NORTH-WEST OF SOUTHAMPTON

Hailed as a perfect example of Queen Anne architecture, Mompesson House presents a distinguished façade in this secluded and exclusive neighbourhood – the peaceful, elegant cathedral close. The close is encircled by 14th-century walls which have three sturdy gateways and these are still locked every night.

Mompesson House was built in 1701 for Charles Mompesson, the local Member of Parliament, and was much improved about 40 years later by his brother-in-law (and heir), Charles Longueville, who redecorated the rooms and added the elegant oak staircase and the decorative plasterwork. This is

The pleasant façade of Mompesson looks out on the Cathedral Close

seen at its best around the stairwell, where every surface is covered with intricate scrolls and motifs.

The house is furnished throughout in appropriate style. The dining room, with 18th-century mahogany furniture, has a sparkling array of silver and is set with fine Sèvres and Coalport china. A display cabinet contains lovely Derby and Bow figures, while another huge cabinet houses a display from the collection of 18th-century drinking glasses bequeathed by Mr O Turnbull. There are over 370 items in the collection, and every one is different. The drawing room is the grandest room of all, with not only

The magnificently carved staircase leads up from the entrance hall

some of the best plasterwork and an impressive chimneypiece, but also works from the Watney bequest of Dutch flower paintings. There is a beautiful cut-glass chandelier, and in a fine mahogany cabinet is part of the Bessemer Wright collection of English porcelain.

The Green Room ceiling features an enormous eagle with outspread wings looking down on the fine walnut furniture and a collection of mezzotints and 17th-century stumpwork pictures, while the 'little' drawing room contains a display of photographs and souvenirs of Miss Barbara Townsend, whose family lived here for about 100 years. Its walls are usually covered with blue-and-white Chinese and Delft dishes, but this room often houses temporary exhibitions.

The most recently opened room in the house is the library, which reflects the ownership of Denis Martineau, who donated the property to the National Trust. Sadly, most of the contents had already been dispersed, and the furnishings seen today come mainly from other sources, but in the library there is an architectural drawing of the Royal Crescent in Bath by Martineau, and the décor of this room reflect his taste.

Open from 1 April to October every afternoon, except Thursday and Friday. Tel: 01722 335659.

CHISENBURY PRIORY
Wiltshire

6 MILES (9.5 KM) SOUTH-WEST OF PEWSEY

South of the Wiltshire town of Pewsey, the River Avon cuts a deep valley into the edge of Salisbury Plain. There, in deep countryside, stands Chisenbury Priory, a red-brick house – partly medieval but more predominantly Georgian – set in charming gardens of about 5 acres (2ha), created during the past 15 years by the owners, Mr and Mrs Alastair Robb.

In front of the house two deep, colourful borders frame the entrance court. Lady's mantle, catmint and sage stand in front of acanthus, artemisias and yellow achilleas, while wisteria and even a vine grow against the brick façade. Behind the house, well maintained lawns are flanked by striking brick walls topped with red tiles, and a laburnum tunnel with yew planted against its vertical posts curves across the upper garden. In cottage garden style, roses and clematis clothe the walls, while the tunnel path is bright with rock roses.

A flight of wide steps run through a border which separates the upper

A profusion of colour surrounds a rustic bench in the walled garden

A rampant clematis almost hides the wall

lawn from the lower, and here artemisias and lavender mix with red, pale pink and rose-coloured phlox. Specimen trees grow on the lawn which slopes gently down to a tributary of the Avon. Here, astilbes, hostas, lilies and gunnera enliven the water's edge, while over a flint-and-stone-bridge espaliered fruit trees mark the end of that part of the garden.

Beyond the wall, the character of the gardens undergoes another change, with an extensive wildflower meadow and another cottage border, dominated by hollyhocks underplanted with geraniums, against the wall.

Mrs Robb also has many rare South African plants at Chisenbury, some of which are tender and kept in pots so that they can be moved into the greenhouse during the winter. Many of the plants that the visitor will have admired during a tour of the garden are propagated here and can be bought, as can a light, white wine made from the Chisenbury vines. These little touches add much to a beautiful garden which, by its diversity of habitat and charming planting, already has much to commend it.

Open on selected days between May and September.

Few prominent families with such a long history are without in the occasional black sheep. For the Herberts, this was the 7th Earl, who not only sank the family into debt but was twice accused of murder. Eventually found guilty of manslaughter, he was incarcerated in the Tower.

WILTON HOUSE
Wiltshire

WILTON, 3 MILES (4.8 KM) WEST OF SALISBURY

Below, the Palladian bridge across the Nadder

W ilton, the home of a particularly interesting family, is a beautiful house, full of beautiful things. The Herberts, Earls of Pembroke, have been here since the estate was given to William, the 1st Earl, by Henry VIII after his dissolution of the monasteries, and successive generations have cherished their home and built up a wonderful collection of works of art. Their interest in the arts is apparent the moment visitors enter the front hall, for there to greet them is a statue of Shakespeare – the bard received patronage from brothers William and Philip Herbert and dedicated the first folio edition of his plays to them. This involvement in the arts has continued to the present day, for the present (17th) earl is a film director and his father was a trustee of the National Gallery, among other similar offices.

The early Herberts tended to marry the sisters of prominent figures of their time – the 1st Earl married the sister of Catherine Parr, sixth wife of Henry VIII, which played some part in his rapid rise at Court. His son Henry, the 2nd Earl, married the sister of Lady

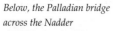

Jane Grey, but this marriage was annulled when the Grey family fell from grace; his second wife was the sister of Sir Philip Sidney, the great Elizabethan poet.

After a disastrous fire in the 17th century much of the house was rebuilt to designs by Inigo Jones. His masterpiece here is the magnificent Double Cube Room which has a superb painted ceiling, gilded plasterwork and fine furniture – and every painting is by Van Dyck, or from his studio. The Single Cube Room is equally sumptuous but smaller, measuring 30ft (9m) in every direction. The Colonnade Room, formerly the state bedroom, is more delicate and houses family portraits by Reynolds. In complete contrast, the large smoking room is fairly plain, except for its elaborate Chippendale cabinet and the delightful collection of 55 paintings of the Spanish *haute école* riding school. The Gothic hall and upper cloisters are different again – part of the work completed in the early 19th century by James Wyatt.

The old riding school at Wilton has now been converted into the Exhibition Hall, where an entertaining film on the lives of the Earls of Pembroke may be seen. After the grandeur of Wilton's state apartments, the reconstructed Tudor kitchen gives an insight into the realities of life in those days.

Open from 3 April to 3 November, daily. Tel: 01722 743115.

Steeped in older history, Wilton was also the unlikely setting of the Southern Headquarters for the D-Day Landings

Tradition has it that the first performances of *Twelfth Night* and *As You Like It* were performed at Wilton by Shakespeare himself and his own company of players.

Old weavers' cottages beside the By Brook

CASTLE COMBE
Wiltshire

6 MILES (9.5 KM) NORTH-WEST OF CHIPPENHAM

The Blanket Brothers

The story goes that two Castle Combe brothers by the name of Blanket, finding their weavers' cottage alongside Pack Bridge somewhat chilly, wove a heavy, raised nap cloth which they wrapped around themselves at night for warmth. Others followed suit, naming their new bedcloth after the brothers.

An especially pretty village set in a hollow on the southern edge of the Cotswolds, Castle Combe owes its name to the fortification built here, first by the Romans, then by the Saxons and finally by Walter de Dunstanville, a Norman. Little remains of his castle but he has a splendid tomb in the church, which is itself a fine example of Gothic architecture, built largely on the wealth of the local clothiers. Near by is their 15th-century market cross, its hipped stone roof supported by four heavy posts. The honeyed-stone weavers' cottages, with typical steep, gabled roofs of Cotswold stone tiles, run down the hill to the By Brook. The bigger houses include the old manor house, now a hotel. The old court house may be distinguished by its overhung, half-timbered upper storey. Behind is the old gaol, a wattle-and-daub building now doing time as a shed. There is a stone dovecote and, beyond, the triple-arched packhorse bridge over the By Brook. Castle Combe is popular with visitors, but thankfully their cars are banished to the outskirts and this intimate and well-kept Cotswold village manages to retain its charm and tranquillity.

STANWAY HOUSE
Gloucestershire

STANWAY, 3 MILES (5 KM) NORTH-EAST OF WINCHCOMBE

New stables were built at Stanway in 1859. The original block, to the east of the barn and next to the churchyard, was abandoned because worshippers were disturbed by 'the oaths of the strappers'.

Built of golden limestone when Queen Elizabeth I was on the throne, Stanway House is not only an outstanding example of Jacobean architecture, it is also a fascinating portrayal of the development of the manor house of a Cotswold squire. Richard Tracy, whose family had owned land in the county since before the Conquest, obtained the lease from the Abbot of Tewkesbury in 1530 – the only time that Stanway has changed hands in the last 1,260 years. It is now the home of Lord and Lady Neidpath whose ancestor, Lord Elcho, married the last Tracy heiress. It is said that he died of an overdose of punch.

There is a sense of continuity at Stanway; it is still very much a lived-in family home and remains the heart of the community. Having resisted the temptation to sell off its cottages, it is one of very few estates to which tenants bring their rent in person on a quarterly basis, handing over the sums due at a 250-year-old table in the Audit Room. The tour of this beautiful house is taken under the watchful eye of generations of family portraits, people who have helped to preserve and perpetuate what is one of the most romantic houses in Britain.

Open from June to September on selected afternoons. Tel: 01386 584469.

The ornate gatehouse at Stanway is beautifully decorated with a shell motif

THE SLAUGHTERS
Gloucestershire

10 MILES (16 KM) WEST OF CHIPPING NORTON

*I*n the heart of the lush Cotswold countryside, the two villages of Lower and Upper Slaughter make a pretty pair. If they are much photographed it is not without justification, for they have a character and charm that belies their gruesome-sounding name. In fact, 'slaughter' is derived from a word meaning no more than 'marshy place'. The River Eye runs through both villages, flowing under picturesque stone footbridges and alongside typically mellow, honey-coloured cottages and houses. In both, the buildings are of the local oolitic limestone, many dating back to the great period of stone building from the mid-16th to the mid-17th century. Most of the roofs are stone-tiled, with gables or dormers, and many of the windows are stone-mullioned, in true Cotswold style.

In Lower Slaughter the red-brick chimney of an early 19th-century corn mill stands out in contrast to the stone-tiled roofs, its waterwheel still intact. The main street runs alongside the river, trees shading the grassy bank

Lower Slaughter, where the River Eye flows broad and shallow

opposite the picture postcard row of houses. Near the church is the former manor house, built in the 17th century for the Whitmore family who continued to be active here until the 1960s. Its dovecote, 16th-century and built like a Cotswold cottage, is one of the largest in the county. But there are lovely houses at every turn. The church has medieval origins but was reconstructed in the 1860s for Charles Shapland Whitmore by Benjamin Ferry. The spire is notable for its fibreglass tip, put into position by a helicopter in the 1960s.

A mile away upstream, the village of Upper Slaughter stands on a grassy hill overlooking the Slaughter Brook, and in among its cluster of cottages and houses are the remains of a Norman motte-and-bailey castle that once dominated the village. Several Norman features survived

19th-century restoration work in the church. Other items of interest here include brasses to the De Slaughter family, who owned the old manor house in the 16th century, and the canopied mortuary chapel of the Reverend F E Witts (d.1854), author of *The Diary of a Cotswold Parson*. His son and grandson succeeded him in the parsonage, now the Lords of the Manor Hotel, and most of the memorials are to the Witts family. Many features of the village remain as they are described in the diary. The group of cottages in the open square, near the churchyard, was remodelled in 1906 by Sir Edwin Lutyens, but since then there has been virtually no new building and the village remains completely in traditional style.

Upper Slaughter: splashes of colour sing out against the mellowed Cotswold stone

BERKELEY CASTLE
Gloucestershire

BERKELEY, 10 MILES (16 KM) SOUTH-WEST OF STROUD

Secluded Berkeley Castle, near the banks of the River Severn, was the site of one of the most infamous of all medieval murders. By 1327, Queen Isabella and her lover, the powerful baron Roger Mortimer, had wrested the crown from Edward II and were running the country. Edward was taken secretly to Berkeley Castle in April 1327, where attempts were made to starve him to death. Dead animals were also thrown into a pit in his room in the hope that the smell would make him sicken and die. But Edward was a strong man and Isabella saw that more drastic measures were necessary. In September, according to tradition, the unfortunate king was murdered by having a red-hot poker thrust into his bowels.

Although the chamber in which Edward is said to have been imprisoned remains, most of the castle dates from the mid 14th century and has survived essentially unchanged since then. It is a great palace-fortress built around a courtyard. Many of Berkeley's rooms are open to visitors, displaying some beautiful furnishings. One room contains furniture said to have belonged to Sir Francis Drake, while the magnificent Great Hall has a superb timber roof dating from the 14th century.

Open April to September, daily except Mondays, and Sunday afternoons in October. Tel: 01453 810332.

Serene Berkeley Castle was the scene of an appalling murder

Village corner, Duntisbourne Abbots

DUNTISBOURNE ABBOTS
Gloucestershire

6 MILES (9.5 KM) NORTH-WEST OF CIRENCESTER

Duntisbourne Abbots is the most northerly of a group of four Duntisbournes. As picturesque as many another Cotswold village, they also have strong associations with the followers of William Morris, who first popularised the Cotswolds. In the parish of Duntisbourne Rouse, to the south-west of the village, lies Pinbury Park, where Ernest Gimson, brilliant interpreter of the Arts and Crafts movement, and his fellow designer-craftsmen, the Barnsley brothers, came to live at the beginning of the century. Cotswold Farm, near Duntisbourne Abbots, was enlarged by Sidney Barnsley in 1926 and has a window by Edward Burne-Jones. In medieval times Duntisbourne Abbots, as indicated by its name, belonged to the Abbot of Gloucester. His mainly Norman but much restored church is approached through a lych-gate, past some good table tombs. Better known is the small church at Duntisbourne Rouse, which has Saxon origins. Making use of the slope on which it stands, the Normans built a crypt under the chancel. The little tower has a saddleback roof and the medieval misericords are to be relished. Duntisbourne Leer, one of several places in the valley where the River Churn has to be forded, and Middle Duntisbourne complete this beautifully situated quartet of mellow Cotswold villages.

FRAMPTON ON SEVERN
Gloucestershire

8 MILES (13 KM) SOUTH OF GLOUCESTER

One of the prerequisites of a perfect village is a green, but few can rival Frampton's. Its 22 acres (9ha), divided by the road that runs through the village, make it one of England's largest, and three ponds and a cricket pitch lie within it. Known as Rosamund's Green, it lends added dignity to the half-timbered and Georgian houses that line its sides. Henry II's mistress, 'Fair Rosamund', Jane Clifford, is said to have been born here. Kept by Henry in a house in Woodstock surrounded by a maze, she is reputed to have been poisoned by Henry's Queen Eleanor, who found her way through the maze by following a thread of the king's cloak.

The seat of the Clifford family is Frampton Court, the most imposing house on the green, though partly hidden by trees. Built in the 1730s in Vanbrugh style, probably by John Strachan of Bristol, it has low wings on either side and handsome chimneys. In the 1980s a beautiful collection of Victorian flower paintings, done by lady members of the family, was discovered in an attic and published as *The Frampton Flora*. Visible from the road is William Halfpenny's 'Strawberry Hill' Gothic orangery, with pretty ogee windows. In front of it, but not visible from the green, is a rectangular canal. On the other side of the green is the family's 15th-century,

Manor Farm

partly half-timbered manor house. Further down the green the houses are smaller and less spaced out, but none the less attractive, some gabled and thatched. Eventually the road bends away from the green to wind through the rest of the village, finally reaching the church, which is set apart from the village beside the Sharpness Canal. The canal-keeper's Doric-style house is not far away and boats pass within yards of the church. It dates mainly from the 14th century, with some 15th-century additions, and with most of its windows being of clear glass it is pleasantly light and airy. There is some medieval glass and the lead font is one of six similar ones surviving in Gloucestershire dated to around 1250–75. There are some notable monuments, particularly the tablet made by John Pearce, 'statuary and diagraphist', in memory of his brothers.

A Georgian house on Rosamund's Green

DEAN FOREST RAILWAY
Gloucestershire

LYDNEY, 9 MILES (14.5 KM) NORTH-EAST OF CHEPSTOW

Coal and iron ore have been mined in the Forest of Dean since before Roman times. By the late 18th century crude waggon-ways were being built to transport the minerals out of the forest, and some of these were later converted into steam-worked railways. The line of the Dean Forest Railway was one of them. It started as a horse-drawn tramway in 1810, built by the Severn & Wye Railway, and was gradually converted to steam traction and railway standards. The 3½-mile (5km) section operated by the Dean Forest Railway is the last of innumerable lines into the Forest, and runs from Lydney Junction to Norchard, where the main centre has been established.

That simple description belies the Herculean task of its creation on the site of a colliery that once employed 400 men. By the time the Dean Forest Railway began work, both colliery and

railway were returning to the forest, calling for navvying on a scale seldom equalled in preservation. All buildings had disappeared, so every structure has had to be located, bought, dismantled, transported and re-erected: a signal box from Gloucester, a platform from Chippenham, a station building from deeper in the forest. Equally, the Dean Forest's engines have had to be restored from a dire condition, and its principal locomotive, a gleaming black Great Western Railway Pannier tank, is another resurrection from the scrapyard at Barry.

As trains edge into the thickly wooded valley the scenery is redolent of an older England, before such large expanses of deciduous forests were felled for development, bisected by motorways or reduced in size to become country parks, shorn of their natural state. The Dean Forest Railway hopes to extend further into the forest

*Concentration on
the footplate*

to Parkend and perhaps beyond, which will permit many to reach walks in the Forest without use of cars. There is also the prospect of the line reaching the Dean Heritage Centre through the fourth oldest railway tunnel in the country, if not the world – the 1064yd (973m) long Haie Tunnel, which opened in 1809.

Train service: Sundays from April to September; also Wednesdays from June to August and Thursdays in August. Santa specials. Tel: 01594 843423.

GWR Pannier tank No 9681 (built in 1949) rounding a bend

HIDCOTE MANOR GARDEN
Gloucestershire

4 MILES (6.5 KM) NORTH-EAST OF CHIPPING CAMPDEN

One of the most beautiful of English gardens, Hidcote Manor is the creation of one remarkable man, Major Lawrence Johnston. Born in Paris of American parents, Johnston grew up in France, and one can see in the formal arrangement of the series of outdoor 'rooms' in the garden the influence, perhaps, of Le Nôtre, as well as of his own architectural training.

Certainly he inherited what was virtually an empty site in 1907, with the exception of a clump of beeches and a fine cedar. His instincts for formality, however, were overlaid both by his wish to re-create the beauties of the traditional cottage garden so evocatively captured in the paintings of Helen Allingham, and by his plant-hunting expeditions to South Africa in 1927 with Major Collingwood Ingram, and in 1931 to Yunnan in China with George Forrest.

Lawrence Johnston's ideas have so often been copied that it is hard to imagine what a novel conception Hidcote must have been in 1914. The tapestry colours of the mixed holly, yew, box and beech hedge around the Fuchsia Garden, the copper beech and hornbeam hedge enclosing the Circle, the different textures of the yew and the holly alongside each other, and the tall, clipped yew hedges surrounding the Theatre Lawn, are now accepted style. But how remarkable they must have been at the time, and what diversity they give to Hidcote today.

The main axis of the garden runs

Left, a profusion of greenery, and below, the more formal White Garden at Hidcote

Lawrence Johnston was influenced by the paintings of Helen Allingham, as may be observed from this riot of sweet peas before the house

from the original cedar of Lebanon, which shades the Old Garden, through the Cottage Borders, the Circle and the Red Borders, and into the Stilt Garden. This formal composition lies alongside the Theatre Lawn, bordered by yew and featuring a raised, circular grass stage crowned by an old beech. The Stilt Garden can be approached through a gap in the yew hedge, and consists of double rows of pleached hornbeams which join at both ends. Through a little brick pavilion you can see the Long Walk running away at right angles, cunningly crossing a little stream as it makes its way to the southern boundary of the garden.

The Red Borders are boldly planted with dark-red cherries, cannas and hemerocallis, while the borders in front of the house are filled with flowers in the Allingham manner, but with the skilful colour harmony associated with Gertrude Jekyll. The central border is pink and mauve with campanula 'Hidcote Amethyst', a purple hibiscus, irises and potentillas, phloxes and peonies, while the northern border is mainly blue and white, and includes clematis, abutilon, philadelphus and the yellow climbing rose, 'Lawrence Johnston'. In the south border there are rhododendrons and the white pendulous *Magnolia sinensis*, as well as poppies and hydrangeas climbing over the walls.

The view from the Circle through the Fuchsia Garden, with its colourful beds surrounded by low box hedges, is one of Hidcote's most striking compositions. The Bathing Pool, despite its name, was designed purely for its visual effect and the circular pond is provided with a stone surround for sitting on, while a magnolia, the rose 'Fruhlingsgold' and drooping sedges are given an additional drama by the surrounding dark-green yew hedges. Many of the plants in the lush Stream Garden come from China, Tibet and Japan, including unusual varieties of camellia and rhododendron, as well as bog arums, giant lilies and *Gunnera manicata*. In

Mrs Winthrop's Garden, designed by Johnston for his mother, the theme is yellow with lilies, peonies, golden lysimachia and *Lonicera nitida* 'Baggesen's Gold'. The Pillar Garden, too, is filled with peonies, and contrast is provided in spring by the magnolias, and in summer by alliums and lilac.

Much of the charm of Hidcote derives from the contrast between formal layout and subtle planting. The colour harmony of the beds and the setting of the stone house in the midst of wonderful Gloucestershire countryside is guaranteed to bring the visitor back to the garden again and again.

Open from April to October, on selected days . Tel: 01386 438333.

A border rich in red flowers and foliage leads to steps and an inviting open gate

INDEX